Kibbeh (page 100)

Upside Down Rice
Casserole (page 114)

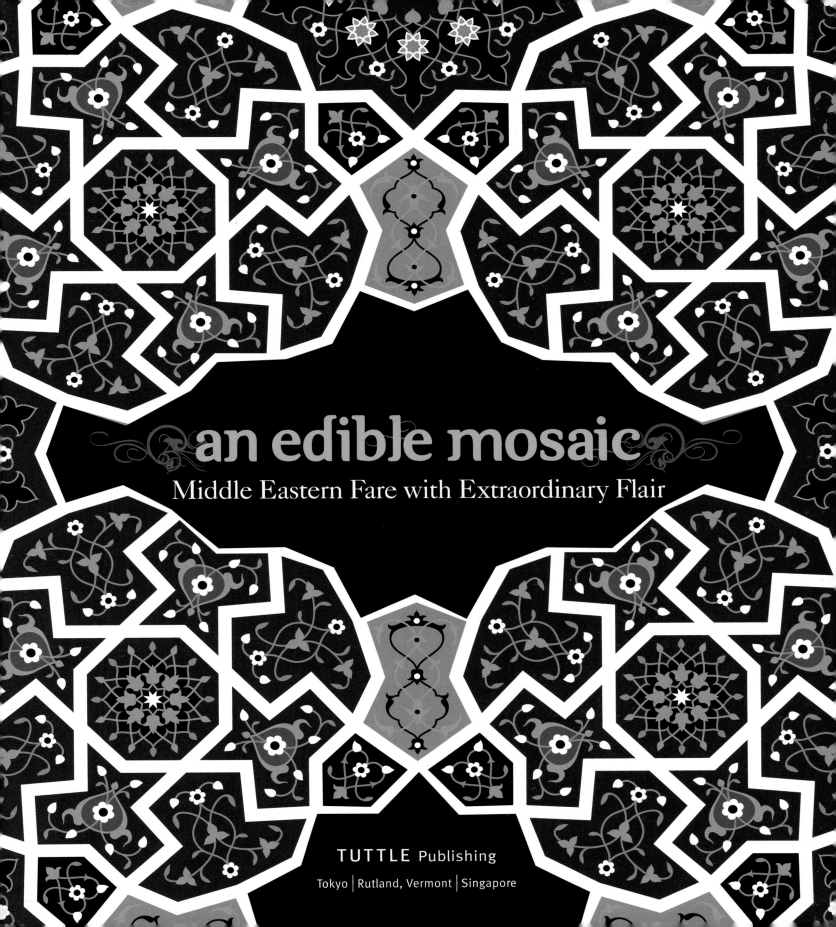

an edible mosaic

Middle Eastern Fare with Extraordinary Flair

TUTTLE Publishing

Tokyo | Rutland, Vermont | Singapore

Contents

Foreword by Lorraine Elliott

I first met Faith a few years ago when I stumbled across her blog. And by meeting her I do mean in the online sense. I have never seen her in person. we live in two completely different and far away countries but that mattered not a jot. I felt like I knew her and that she and I had so much in common. I would read her blog and exclaim how I had felt the very same way about a topic or had the same experience.

The number of times that we both commented that we were "sisters" was innumerable and her blog stood out to me and she stood out to me as someone that I could count as a friend even though we technically hadn't met. It had been years since I visited New York and she has never visited Australia. The Internet and blogosphere is funny and charming like that.

Apart from the common reactions to things, I loved her recipes, many of which I have tried. Middle Eastern cuisine is one that I love to eat but have not had much experience preparing. And this is where Faith comes in, not just to me but to the many thousands of readers that she has. Knowing that she had gained all of her knowledge through the years from her mother-in-law, overriding a language barrier to prepare recipes that her Middle Eastern husband Mike (who I also feel like I know so well!) would like, makes me treasure them even more.

It's passion for learning and passion for a culture that makes one want to learn more about its cuisine. Family recipes are like little golden wrapped treasures held together by delicate webs and gossamer. It can be a challenge to get to the core of them while traversing vague measurements and getting to know mysterious but exciting ingredients. But they are worth the time to get to know because not only are the flavors wonderful, there is also depth and gravity given to them with the family history and it is a privilege for us to have access to these recipes.

Practically speaking, I appreciate the way that she approaches Middle Eastern cuisine. Like those of us that don't come from the culture but appreciate it, no question is too silly or basic and she explains the basics to us much like a good friend would. I never knew that pomegranate molasses is great on a falafel sandwich but you bet I'll be drizzling that the next time I have one!

We all know that food is more than a source of fuel and energy and that it brings people together. It can also provide comfort for those eating and also making it a pride of place whenever there is a celebration. Faith imbues her recipes with warmth and comfort and I look at her as a good friend who imparts her most treasured secrets to those lucky enough to have found her.

Lorraine

Lorraine Elliott
www.notquitenigella.com

Cauliflower Meat
Sauce (page 110)

My Passion for Middle Eastern Cooking

Middle Eastern fare isn't the cuisine I grew up eating. Actually, until about six years ago, the only Middle Eastern foods I had ever eaten were hummus, falafel, shish kebab, and baklava… and looking back, I can tell you that everything I ate up until that point was in no way authentic. So, how did I end up with such a passion for Middle Eastern cuisine?

My husband, Mike, is Middle Eastern; actually, his father is Palestinian and his mother is Syrian; he was born in Kuwait, raised in Syria, and went to college in Jordan. Suffice to say he was raised on Middle Eastern fare and, being the picky eater he is, he doesn't care for foods unless his mom makes it. This, of course, meant that when Mike and I first got married I had to learn how to cook authentic Middle Eastern food.

Mike and I were married in the Middle East, and we lived there for the first six months of our marriage. During this time I had the opportunity to experience firsthand the magic of Middle Eastern cuisine. I saw how a spectacular dish can start with just an ordinary ingredient…

that is, if you add the right combination of spices, and give it the time and effort to cook it properly with the passion and attention it deserves, or as they say in Arabic, *nefus ala el ekel* (literally meaning to "have breath that is good for food"). I discovered even more exotic and wonderful foods the longer I stayed in Syria and I even started to enjoy Middle Eastern foods that I didn't care for originally, like slimy green soup (*Molokhia*) and super tangy yogurt cheese (*Labneh*). As I was experiencing all these new foods, I was also learning how to cook them from my mother-in-law, Sahar, a fantastic cook, who, in true Syrian tradition, knew her way around the kitchen before the age of ten. The only way to learn how to cook from authentic old world cooks is to watch them in action. Nothing is written down, there are no cooking times, very few enumerated steps, and certainly no measurements. I remember one night Mike requested I make him rice pudding, so he asked his mom for the recipe. This is the translation of what she told him: "Cook some rice and warm some milk. Add cornstarch and sugar and boil. Make sure to add rosewater." When I asked how much milk, the answer was "as much as you want to make." And what about the rice? "A small coffee cup of rice." Keep in mind that Middle Eastern coffee, like espresso, is served in tiny demitasse cups…luckily I knew this before I made the pudding! Those were only the start of my questions though. From then on, I realized that if I wanted to learn how to cook Middle Eastern food I would have to watch Sahar. But even this wasn't as easy as it sounds.

There was a language barrier between Sahar and I: she spoke only a little English and I spoke even less Arabic. In the beginning, much of our time together in the kitchen was spent pointing to ingredients and both excitedly exclaiming what they were. Then I would watch her cook and, as she was working, I took the time to intricately write down ingredients, measurements, methods, steps, and cooking times. Finally, it got to the point where I had mastered a few recipes and I was the one making family meals…and with a family of about ten this was no small feat! As I fell in love with Middle Eastern cuisine and culture, learning the art of Middle Eastern cooking became a passion for me. When Mike and I left the Middle East after spending six months there, I left with a knowledge of and a great appreciation for Middle Eastern fare; more than that though, I truly felt like I had been accepted into his family.

Since then I've had the opportunity to travel to the Middle East four other times. After mastering a number of basic recipes and techniques, I've been able to delve even deeper into the cuisine and culture of the region, which has given me an even deeper passion for Middle Eastern fare.

When Mike and I arrived in the U.S., I felt prepared to make him his favorite Middle Eastern foods; actually, by then my passion for cooking had grown immensely and I began to take every opportunity to learn about new dishes, techniques, and regional cuisines. As my love for cooking grew, so did my talent. I began planning special occasion menus for my family, which evolved into family and friends asking me to cater events for them. After making a Mother's Day meal for my mom in 2009, I decided to start a food blog (www.AnEdibleMosaic.com) to share the meal that I had made for her. In initiating my blog, I hoped to be an inspiration to home cooks who were looking for a little bit of encouragement to experiment in the kitchen (because after all, I'm a home cook myself…and if I can do it, so can they!). My other reason for starting *An Edible Mosaic* was to have a venue to share the wealth of information I had learned about Middle Eastern cuisine. Authentic old world recipes are typically shared orally and aren't put into writing, but since I had the good fortune of being able to watch a master Middle Eastern cook in the kitchen, I knew this information had to be memorialized and shared with the world.

Through this book, I'm sharing the recipes that I've lovingly learned to make in hopes that they become new favorites and the basis of new traditions for other families. I'm hoping to show home cooks that Middle Eastern food is not only delicious but also attainable, and goes well beyond the commonly known Middle Eastern favorites. Another of my aspirations for this book is that it serves as a written collection of authentic Middle Eastern fare for those who are looking for traditional recipes. I think it will be indispensible to people who have traveled to the Middle East or have married into a Middle Eastern family and want to be able to replicate authentic Middle Eastern recipes at home. My final goal is that this book teaches a bit of Middle Eastern culture along with cuisine, as the two are so closely intertwined.

May you always have a healthy appetite. *Saha (to your health)!*

Faith Gorsky
author of *An Edible Mosaic*

Cooking Tips and Techniques

This section is meant as a guide for some of the most commonly used techniques in Middle Eastern cooking. As I learned how to cook, I was surprised that even a small amount of extra effort can make a huge difference in a finished product. Brining chicken, for example, requires minimal effort and you will be able to taste the difference from the first bite: not only is brined chicken more tender and juicy, but it tastes fresher and has less of a fishy flavor than non brined chicken. This section also shows you that some kitchen tasks are much easier to do at home than you might have thought. For example, I used to buy blanched almonds at the grocery store before I realized how easy it is to blanch them at home (and it saves money too!). And there are other tasks that I did well enough (ahem, cooking eggplant) and was happy with the results, but wasn't very impressed by the food's flavor until I learned the proper way to handle it (like giving it a little time alone with some salt). Little tricks like these will transform your food from good to fantastic.

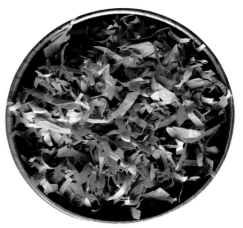

Chiffonading Herbs: This technique is used to shred herbs into thin, confetti-like strips. The purpose of this technique is to keep the herbs as fresh and crisp as possible, with minimal wilting or bruising. For most salads that use minced herbs such as Middle Eastern Salad (page 47) and Colorful Cabbage with Lemony Salad Dressing (page 40), a regular mincing technique works perfectly fine, and for most *cooked* dishes that contain minced herbs, like Sautéed Greens and Cilantro (page 58) and Cauliflower Meat Sauce (page 110), I'll go one step further and say that a Mincing Knife/Mezzaluna (page 16) does a decent mincing job. However, there are a few dishes where the integrity of the herb is of utmost importance and so chiffonading is the best technique; one such dish is Tabbouleh (page 44). Before chiffonading any herb, wash the herb and let it dry completely (water can cause it to blacken quicker). To cut up large, flat-leafed herbs (such as mint, basil, and sage), pick the leaves off their stems and stack about eight to ten leaves; tightly roll the stack lengthwise into a cigar shape, then use a sharp paring knife to thinly slice across the cigar, creating little ribbons. Parsley is a bit more difficult to chiffonade since the leaves are smaller and more irregularly shaped; don't let this deter you though, once you get the hang of it, it really will be quick work. The method for chiffonading parsley is described in the recipe for Tabbouleh.

Blanching Almonds: Blanched almonds are frequently used as a garnish for both sweet and savory dishes. They are wonderful on top of puddings or as a garnish for other desserts, like Coconut Semolina Cake (Harissa) (page 130), or sautéed up in a little bit of clarified butter or olive oil, they add flavor and crunch to rice dishes like Upside-Down Rice Casserole (Maqluba) (page 114) and Baked Chicken with Red Rice Pilaf (Kebseh) (page 96). Blanched almonds are commonly available at grocery stores, but in a pinch it's good to know how to make them at home. There are four steps to the process: (1) place fresh, shelled (raw and unsalted) almonds in a heat-safe bowl; (2) pour in enough boiling water to fully cover the almonds; (3) let the almonds sit for 1 minute, then pour into a mesh sieve, rinse under cold water, and drain; and (4) hold one almond at the wide end between your thumb and forefinger and gently squeeze—the skin should slip right off. (*Note:* If your almonds aren't the freshest, you can use a slightly different method to blanch them. Pour them into a saucepan, add enough water to cover, and bring up to a rolling boil. Boil 1 minute, then pour into a mesh sieve, rinse under cold water, and drain. The skins should slip right off.) Blanching can cause almonds to lose a bit of their crispness, as they tend to absorb water. To dry them out, pat them dry with paper towels or a clean kitchen towel, and then spread them in an even layer on a large baking pan. Let them sit in a sunny spot for a full day, or transfer them to an oven that has been preheated to 200°F (95°C) and then turned off. Once dried, store blanched almonds in the freezer.

Cooking Dried Beans and Lentils: As a general rule of thumb, I use canned beans but dried lentils (which cook much quicker than dried beans) for cooking. Of course, there are a few recipes for which dried beans are noticeably better, such as Hummus (page 79) and Falafel (page 81), and for those select few I take the extra time to cook dried beans. If you want to use dried beans be sure to plan ahead, since most should be soaked in cold water for 12 to 24 hours, during which time the beans will swell as they absorb water. (If you're really pressed for time, here's a trick that my mom taught me: add the [unsoaked] beans to a large pot and cover with water; bring up to a boil, boil 3 minutes, then turn the heat off, cover the pot and let the beans sit for one hour; drain and proceed with cooking the beans.) After soaking, drain the beans and add them to a large pot with fresh water; bring them to a boil over high heat, then turn the heat down slightly and boil until they're tender, adding more water as necessary so that they are immersed, (the exact amount of time will vary depending on several factors, including what kind of bean you're using, how old the beans are, and even the weather); this generally takes one to two hours for chickpeas. (Don't add salt or acid—such as lemon juice, tomato, or vinegar —to the water as the beans cook, since these can cause the skins to toughen; instead, season the beans once they're tender.) Also, during the cooking process, the skin on the beans will sometimes come off; you can pick through the beans to remove it if you want. This step is fairly time-consuming and is optional; I may or may not do it depending on how I plan to use the beans. However, I've noticed that when I take the time to pick out the skins when I make the Hummus, I end up with a much creamier consistency. Here are the general equivalent measurements for canned and dried beans: 1 (approximately 16 oz/500 g) can of beans = 1¾ cups = ⅔ cup (4¾ oz/135 g) dry beans.

Cooking Eggplant: First things first, when you're buying your eggplant, look for smaller fruits rather than larger ones, since they will usually be less bitter and have fewer seeds. Eggplant should be smooth and shiny, and feel heavy for its size. If it's ripe, when you gently press a finger into it, the eggplant should give a bit but the indentation should spring back; if the flesh doesn't spring back, it's probably over-ripe and if it doesn't give at all, it's probably under-ripe. If eggplant is being roasted whole, such as for Roasted Eggplant Salad (page 44) or Eggplant Dip (page 64), it should not be peeled; other than that, peeling eggplant is based generally on personal preference. I usually peel larger ones and don't peel smaller ones, but sometimes I partially peel them for a striped appearance. After peeling, slice the eggplant into about ¼ to ½-inch (6 mm to 1.25 cm) thick slices; salt both sides of each slice, place the eggplant in a colander, and put the colander in the sink for 30 minutes. During this time you will notice a brownish liquid seep out (this is normal), which will help reduce the eggplant's bitterness. After that, rinse the eggplant under cold running water; gently wring it out, and then pat it dry. At this point, the eggplant can be deep or shallow-fried, or brushed with a little olive oil and grilled or broiled until golden on both sides. Prepared this way, eggplant is perfect for Fried Eggplant with Garlic and Parsley Dressing (page 53) or Upside-Down Rice Casserole (page 114).

Cooking with Yogurt: Yogurt is often used to make wonderfully tangy, yet creamy soups like Lamb and Yogurt Soup (page 109) and sauces such as the sauce in Stuffed Squash in Yogurt Sauce (page 104). The only issue with cooking yogurt is that it has to be given a bit of extra care to prevent curdling. For starters, don't use a fat-free yogurt, since a higher fat content helps prevent curdling; full fat is best but reduced-fat will also work. Making sure your yogurt is at room temperature when you're ready to use it also helps. Use the amount of cornstarch and (sometimes) egg that are specified in each recipe, as these ingredients are added to both thicken and stabilize the yogurt. Lastly, yogurt should always be cooked gently (medium heat or lower is best), while being stirred *constantly* in one direction with a wooden spoon.

Frying Basics: Middle Eastern cooks don't seem to shy away from deep or shallow frying, since many recipes—from Fried Eggplant with Garlic and Parsley Dressing (page 53) to Falafel (page 81) to Spicy Potatoes (page 57)—all contain fried components. If you follow proper frying procedures, food doesn't absorb an excessive amount of oil; instead, you're left with a crispy exterior and tender interior. When you fry, make sure to choose the right oil; in Middle Eastern cooking, good quality corn oil is typically used for frying, but any good oil with a high smoke point will work. The next point to consider is what vessel to fry in; if you're deep-frying look for a large heavy-bottomed pot with deep sides (you can fill it up about one-third to one-half of the way with oil) and if you're shallow-frying, a large skillet (preferably with a heavy bottom) will work (about ½ inch / 1.25 cm) of oil in the bottom of the skillet is usually perfect. Make sure the oil is up to temperature before adding the food; for most recipes, 350 to 375°F (175 to 190°C) is just right, and ensure your food is patted completely dry before adding

Hollowing Out Vegetables to Stuff: In Middle Eastern cuisine, about any vegetable is stuffed. A few favorites are tomatoes, small bell peppers, cabbage, grape leaves, small potatoes, baby eggplants, and marrow squashes (see Marrow Squash, page 120). If you can't find marrow squash, zucchini is a good substitute; look for small zucchini, about 8 to 10 inches (20 to 25 cm) long that are as straight as possible, which can be cut in half so that each half can be hollowed out. Cabbage and grape leaves don't need to be hollowed out; they are simply rolled up tightly with stuffing. Tomatoes and bell peppers are easy to hollow out: just cut off the top where the stem is and scoop the insides out. To hollow out potatoes, eggplant, and marrow squash (or zucchini), you will need a vegetable corer (page 17). For marrow squash, zucchini, or eggplant, trim off both the stem and blossom ends. Hold the fruit in one hand and insert a vegetable corer into the center, gently rotating the fruit so it turns around the corer; remove the corer, set the pulp aside, and continue gently scraping the inside of fruit; continue this way until you have a shell about ¼ inch (6 mm) thick. For potatoes, choose medium-sized vegetables and peel them before you start coring; core them the same way you would eggplant, zucchini, or marrow squash, but leave the shell about ½ inch (1.25 cm) thick. The insides that are scooped out can be added to soups, made into dips, or omelets like the Zucchini Fritters on page 65.

it. When you (carefully) add the food, be sure not to overcrowd the pan. (This will drop the temperature too much, causing your food to be soggy and greasy.) When your food is cooked, transfer it immediately to a paper towel-lined plate to drain any excess oil; also, this is the best time to salt the food since it will be absorbed best (other than eggplant, which is salted before frying to reduce the bitterness; see Cooking Eggplant on page 11). A very useful tool for frying is the spider strainer (page 17) and

also, something called a splatter guard, which is a circular mesh cover with a handle that is placed on pans when frying to prevent oil from spattering out. Of course, if you really don't want to fry in the traditional way, "oven-frying" is also an option for most foods; in this method, foods are lightly coated in oil and cooked in a hot oven until crisp outside and soft inside. For a description of "oven-frying" as pertaining to cauliflower, see the recipe for Cauliflower Meat Sauce on page 110.

Making Middle Eastern Salads: Salads are a huge part of Middle Eastern cuisine, as some form of raw vegetable is typically present at every meal. For the smaller meals (breakfast and dinner), maza platters usually contain large pieces of vegetables that are picked up and eaten with your hands: whole leaves of crisp Romaine lettuce along with sliced or chunked cucumber and tomato, whole green onion, and quartered white onion. For lunch (the largest and most formal meal of the day), vegetables are usually chopped neatly into salads and eaten as is or spooned on top of rice (if rice is present in the meal). The signature of a Middle Eastern salad in general and a Syrian salad in particular is the precision with which the vegetables are cut. Before being chopped, vegetables are cleaned by soaking them in a large bowl of cold water with a splash of Apple Vinegar (page 26); after this they are rinsed and patted dry. Tomatoes, cucumbers, and white onions are cut into a perfect dice. Green onions (scallions) are thinly sliced and fresh parsley and/or mint are minced with razor-sharp paring knives. Lettuce and/or cabbage are finely shredded into little ribbons. A tart, refreshing dressing, such as the Lemony Mint Salad Dressing on page 28, is mixed and the salad is dressed at the last minute right before eating so the vegetables stay fresh and crisp. As you can imagine, this process can take a while, especially if you're cooking for a crowd; this is why many women use

Making the Perfect Pot of Rice: I remember when making rice was the bane of my existence. After watching my mother-in-law make rice effortlessly, I picked up a few helpful tricks that ensure perfect rice every time. Before you start preparing the rice, get out a saucepan or pot, preferably with a thick bottom (or use a heat diffuser) for cooking the rice. Rinse the rice under running water to remove any talc or excess starch; this will result in fluffier rice. After rinsing, soak the rice for 10 minutes; this makes the rice less brittle so it's less likely to break while cooking, shortens the cooking time, and lets the rice—particularly basmati—expand to its full length. While the rice is soaking, put half a kettle of water on to boil. Drain the rice well after soaking, and then it's ready to be toasted. Toast the rice in a little oil or clarified butter in the pot that you're going to cook it in; it will start to smell amazingly nutty at this point. Add water. The exact amount of water you'll need depends on a few different factors, including how old the rice is, the starch content (including how long the rice was rinsed for), how the rice was harvested and processed, the type of cooking vessel you're cooking it in, the lid you're using, temperature, humidity, etc.; generally though, I start with a little more water than the amount of rice I'm using. Then bring the rice up to a boil, cover the pot, and turn it down to very low. Let the rice cook until it's tender but not mushy and all the water is absorbed (this takes about 10 minutes) without opening the lid; at this point turn off the heat and let the rice sit for 15 minutes. Uncover the rice, fluff it with a fork, and revel in its perfection.

Above: Soaking rice (top); draining rice (middle); and fluffed rice (bottom).

large utility boards, often taking the board to the parlor or guest room with a group of women so she can talk with visiting ladies (neighbors, friends, and family are frequent daytime guests) as

she works. Also, most salads can be made ahead; just chop all the veggies and toss them together as normal, but wait to add the dressing until right before you're ready to serve the salad.

Preparing Chicken: Most chicken recipes in this book require use of a whole chicken; this is generally the best bargain, and what is most commonly used in the Middle East. For most recipes, the chicken must first be butchered. To do so, remove the innards, giblets, head, and neck (most chickens can be purchased this way from the grocery store). Cut out the chicken's backbone by first cutting down one side of it and then down the other; quarter the chicken so you have 2 breasts and 2 thigh/leg pieces, and then cut each breast into 2 pieces, leaving the wing attached. You will end up with 6 pieces total; if you prefer, you can also separate the leg and thigh so you end up with 8 pieces total. Cut away the wing tips and excess fat, leaving the skin on; rinse the chicken and pat it dry. The next step—soaking or brining—is optional but highly recommend. Brining chicken yields juicier, tenderer, and more flavorful result, and it also helps to refresh the meat, removing any "fishy" smells. To brine a whole chicken, butcher the chicken as described above, then put it into a large, non-reactive bowl. Add 1 tablespoon non-iodized salt, 1 tablespoon apple cider vinegar, 1 tablespoon fresh lemon juice, and 4 cups (1 liter) of lukewarm water to a large measuring cup with a pour spout; stir to dissolve, then cool to room temperature. Pour the liquid over the chicken, and then add enough cold water to cover, transfer to the fridge and soak 4 hours (or up to 2 days). Once it's done soaking, rinse the chicken thoroughly under cold running water, pat dry, and proceed with the recipe. Now for cooking the chicken…typically in Middle Eastern cooking, when chicken is served with a meal containing a sauce and/or rice dish, like Roast Chicken with Rice and Vegetable Soup on page 90 or Baked

Putting Together Maza Platters: Maza can have several different meanings, but in this book I'm referring to a variety of different dishes on small plates, served together on one large platter. Usually food served this way is rustically eaten off the tray either with your hands or with flatbread for scooping. This style of eating is common for smaller meals (i.e., breakfast and dinner), and is also used to serve appetizers before lunch (which is the largest meal of the day) or as a snack. So, what goes on a maza platter? It can be anything you like! Breakfast platters may contain eggs (cooked any way), fresh herbs, sliced tomato and/or cucumber, Yogurt Cheese (page 73), Sesame Fudge (page 119), a variety of olives, olive oil, Thyme Spice Mix (page 29), flatbread, and tea. For maza platters served at other times of the day, leftovers are perfect and vegetable dishes are abundant; I've seen many a maza with fried eggplant, like the eggplant made in Fried Eggplant with Garlic and Parsley Dressing on page 53 or a small dish of Okra with Tomatoes in a Fragrant Sauce on page 55 or Spiced Green Beans with Tomatoes on page 59. In general, maza platters don't include meat, unless it's leftovers that had meat, or occasionally a can of tuna, a tin of sardines, or a bit of sliced luncheon meat, such as *mortadella* or *basterma*.

Left: Clockwise From Twelve O'clock: Olive Oil, Fresh Mint Leaves, Flatbread, Yogurt Cheese (page 73), Assorted Olives, Chopped Tomato, and Fresh Green Onion (Scallion); Thyme Spice Mix (page 29) and Sliced Cucumber in the center

Below: Clockwise From Two O'clock: Romaine Lettuce, Baby Tomatoes, Flatbread, Tuna Fish, and Lemon Wedges (center)

Chicken with Red Rice Pilaf on page 96, the chicken is first boiled until fully cooked, and then deep-fried to crisp the skin. The one benefit I can see of this method is that you end up with homemade chicken stock as a by-product of boiling the chicken; however, since good quality stock or even stock cubes are commonly available at grocery stores, I prefer a simpler, one-step method that I think results in juicier, more flavorful chicken: roasting! To roast, preheat oven to 350°F (175°C) and arrange the chicken pieces in a single layer on a large baking sheet. Rub the top with a little olive oil, yogurt, and/or spices (each recipe will specify the quantities) and roast until the juices run clear when poked with a sharp knife, about 50 to 60 minutes. Once roasted, if you want the chicken to have more color, you can broil it for a couple of minutes. (My mother-in-law has recently started using a slightly different method: boiling the chicken as normal, but then placing the chicken in a shallow dish, rubbing the top with a little yogurt, and broiling it until it gets a little color. I think this method is pretty ingenious, but I still prefer the flavor and texture of chicken that has been roasted.) In the end, you can cook the chicken whatever way is easiest for you.

Using a Pressure Cooker: These days most of us are so busy that kitchen shortcuts have become indispensible; even my mother-in-law in Syria (a traditionalist in the kitchen) frequently uses a pressure cooker to save time. A pressure cooker is a special pot with an airtight lid and a vent or pressure release valve (newer models have more safety features and slightly fancier lids). So how does a pressure cooker speed up cooking? Food and liquid are put into the pressure cooker and the lid is sealed on top; the pot is then placed on a heat source. Once the liquid boils, the steam that would normally escape has nowhere to go

Coffee the Middle Eastern Way: What is commonly known as Turkish Coffee (Qaweh Turkiyeh) is drunk all day long in the Middle East; it's what you wake up to, what you drink as an afternoon pick-me-up, and what you serve to guests. (For more information, see Turkish Coffee, page 139.) Traditional Arabic coffee (called *Qaweh Arabi* or *Qaweh Mourra*) is generally reserved for a few special occasions, such as holidays, weddings, and funerals. Green coffee beans are roasted in a pan over a fire and then coarsely ground with cardamom using a large brass mortar and pestle. Water and the ground coffee are added to the pot used for making Arabic Coffee (see Middle Eastern Coffee Pot, page 16), and then placed on the fire to brew. Once the coffee boils, it is typically left to simmer for around 10 minutes, and then it's removed from the heat and steeped for about another 10 minutes. At this point, other spices such as cloves may be added, but sugar and milk are never added. Dates may or may not be offered along with the coffee. A small amount of coffee—usually just enough to cover the bottom of the cup—is poured into a small cup without a handle called a *finjan* (which is about the same size as a demitasse cup). (A small but important note, coffee should be poured from a pot held in the left hand into a cup held in the right; it should always be drunk from the right hand.) Guests are served in the order of their importance and then the host serves himself last. Empty cups are handed back to the host; if the cup is shaken, it signifies to the host that the

drinker is finished. If the cup isn't shaken when it's handed back, it signifies that the drinker would like more coffee. The first time I had this coffee was at a restaurant in Syria; I was quite surprised at its bitterness. I asked a friend about the coffee's bitterness and he told me that it isn't a matter of liking Arabic coffee. He said that in Middle Eastern culture, it's just something you know you'll taste a couple times a year.

since the pressure cooker's lid is airtight; instead, the steam remains trapped and causes the pressure inside the pot to increase. As the pressure increases, so does the temperature at which the liquid boils, allowing foods to cook more quickly (foods cooked under pressure typically cook in about one-third of the time). In Middle Eastern cooking, foods with long simmering times (such as meat, beans, etc.) are well suited for pressure-cooking. (*Note:* Make sure to thoroughly read the manufacturer's instructions before getting started.)

Basic Cooking Tools

Glancing through the list of cooking tools, you'll notice that some are very traditional (mortar and pestle) and others are for today's modern kitchen (think food processor!). Modern kitchen tools and appliances are by no means necessities (that is, if time is not of the essence), since cooking tasks can always be done by hand the traditional way…but these amenities sure do make our lives easier. And on the flip side, traditional tools still have their place too; I use my mortar and pestle nearly every day, even if it's to do nothing more than crush garlic or grind spices. Many of the tools listed here are probably already in your kitchen; others can be found in any department store, and there are a select few that you will probably only be able to find in Middle Eastern stores.

Cookie Molds (Alleb Ma'amoul): There are three different types of mold used for making Date-Filled Cookies (page 118), and each is used for a different filling. The mold for date filling is circular with a flat top, the mold for pistachio filling is circular with a pointed top, and the mold for walnut filling is oval shaped. Some molds are made of plastic, but most are made of wood with intricate carvings inside and a flat rim above the well, which is where you firmly tap on a hard surface to remove the pastry. Most molds are about the same size: the date and pistachio molds are approximately 2 inches (5 cm) in diameter, and the walnut mold is about 2.5 inches x 1.5 inches (6.5 cm x 3.75 cm).

Food Processor (Khulat): This modern-day kitchen tool has become a very handy addition to today's Middle Eastern kitchen. Things that were traditionally made by hand with a mortar and pestle (see page 17), such as Creamy Garlic Sauce on page 24, Eggplant Dip on page 64, and Bell Pepper Walnut Dip on page 72, now take a fraction of the time to make in a food processor.

Large Cutting Board/Utility Board (Methrameh): A large cutting board is handy for so many kitchen tasks; in the Middle Eastern kitchen, a large board is particularly useful for making salads since they frequently have many different components, most of which are meticulously chopped (see Making Middle Eastern Salads, page 12). I prefer sturdy plastic boards over other materials, since they can be thoroughly disinfected; also, I like to keep a separate board for cutting meats and vegetables/fruits.

Middle Eastern Coffee Pot (Della): There are two kinds of pots used: one for traditional/special occasion Arabic coffee (called *Qaweh Arabi* or *Qaweh Mourra*, which means "bitter coffee"), and one for everyday coffee, which is commonly known as Turkish coffee (*Qaweh Turkiyeh*); these pots are called the same thing, but are differentiated by the type of coffee you want to make. The pot used for Arabic coffee comes in many sizes and styles but has a pointed, beak-like spout. The pot used to brew everyday coffee also comes in many sizes and styles, but it's sloped, with a narrower top leading down to a slightly wider base.

Mincing Knife/Mezzaluna (Ferrameh): This knife has a single or double curved blade with a handle on both ends, allowing food (such as herbs or other vegetables) to be minced in a back-and-forth rocking motion. The good thing about this tool is that it typically makes

quick work out of mincing; however, the downside is that it's easy to bruise herbs using it. Generally, if an herb is being added to a cooked dish, such as cilantro to Sautéed Greens and Cilantro on page 58, this tool works just fine, otherwise, herbs should be minced using a regular mincing technique (also see Chiffonading Herbs, page 10). This tool is most frequently used to mince fresh jute mallow to make Roast Chicken with Rice and Vegetable Soup (page 90).

Mortar and Pestle (Mudukka): A mortar is a bowl-shaped object and a pestle is a blunt, elongated object; you need them both to get the job done. Food (such as spices or garlic) is placed into the mortar, and the pestle is used to crush or grind the food, or create an emulsion such as Garlic Mayonnaise (page 24). Both mortars and pestles are usually made out of heavy material, such as stone or hard wood, since this helps grind the food faster. For many purposes nowadays, a Food Processor (page 16) is used instead of a mortar and pestle to save time.

Round Baking Pan (Saynieh): These resemble round cake pans; they are about

2 inches (5 cm) deep and come in a variety of sizes from very small to very, very large. They are useful for cooking any number of things, such as Coconut Semolina Cake (Harissa) (page 130) or Meatballs with Potato in Tomato Sauce (page 113). Extra large pans are also very useful for kneading dough with easy clean up.

Serving Platters (Saynieh): Serving platters come in many different shapes, sizes, and styles. Fancy ones are used to serve guests and plainer ones get more everyday wear. Small platters (*saynieyet qaweh*) are used for serving perhaps an afternoon coffee with a small plate of cookies and larger platters (*saynieyet ak-kel*) are used for serving a rice dish or for arranging a maza spread on it.

Sharp Paring Knife (Sikkeen): This is a smallish knife (typically about 3 to 4 inches/7.5 to 10 cm) long with a smooth edge. The small size of this knife gives a great amount of control to the user, and is used as an all-purpose knife in many Middle Eastern kitchens. To keep her knives sharp, my mother-in-law sharpens them about twice a week on the bottom of a stoneware plate.

Vegetable Corer (Hafara): This tool is a long, narrow blade curved into a half moon shape; it is used to hollow out vegetables such as squash, eggplant, and potato for stuffing. If a vegetable corer isn't available, a narrow, sharp-tipped vegetable peeler or a narrow apple corer may work.

Skewers (Sieakh): These long metal or wooden sticks typically have a sharp tip on one end and a handle on the other; food is threaded on and then grilled. They come in all different shapes and sizes; large flat skewers (as seen on the left side of the photo) work well for kebabs, such as Chicken Kebabs (page 88) and Lamb or Beef Kebabs (page 112), since ground meat is easier to mold onto thicker skewers. Thinner skewers work (shown on the right side of the picture) work well for cooking chunks of meat, like Marinated Chicken Skewers (page 88).

Spider Strainer (Musfieh): This long-handled utensil has a woven-wire or mesh circular basket at one end. It's commonly used to scoop food out of hot oil (when deep-frying) or water (when blanching).

Buying the Right Middle Eastern Ingredients

When it comes to Middle Eastern ingredients you will find that most of the other ingredients used in the recipes in this book are probably already in your pantry/freezer/fridge, or are readily available at your grocery store. And even the ingredients on this list are likely to be found in the regular section of your regular grocery store (like cardamom, dates, and pine nuts), or in your grocery store's "ethnic" or "international" section (like bulgur wheat or fava beans). Some things can be easily made at home (like pomegranate molasses) or substituted (like lemon juice for citric acid, zucchini for marrow squash, other fresh herbs for mint or purslane, or equal parts unsalted butter and canola oil for clarified butter). For the few ingredients that are harder to find check your local Middle Eastern grocery store (see the Resource Guide, page 140).

Apricot Leather (*Qamar al Deen*): The name literally translates to "moon of the religion." It's made from puréed apricots that are spread onto large trays and dried in the sun; the dried sheets of apricot are lightly brushed with oil, folded, and tightly wrapped in plastic to keep them fresh. Apricot leather keeps best stored at room temperature. It can be eaten as candy, made into Apricot Drink (page 138), or Layered Apricot and Milk Pudding (page 120).

Clockwise From Top Right: Whole Sour Black Cherry Pits (*Mahlab*), Ground Sour Black Cherry Pits, Saffron (*Zafaron*), Nigella Seeds (*Habbat al Barakeh*), Sumac (*Sumac*), and Cardamom (*Hale*) (center)

Bulgur Wheat, Fine Grind (Back) and Medium Grind (Front)

Bulgur Wheat (*Burghul*): Typically made from durum wheat, but can also be made from other types of wheat. It is parboiled, stripped of its outer layers of bran, and dried. It is then ground into three different sizes: #1—fine, #2—medium, and #3—coarse. The fine grind is commonly used in Tabbouleh (page 44) and Kibbeh (page 100). Medium or coarse-ground bulgur wheat is prepared similarly to rice in dishes like Lentil and Bulgur Pilaf with Caramelized Onion (page 82).

Cardamom (*Hale*): Cardamom, which is related to ginger, produces green or black pods that contain fragrant black seeds. (*Note*: In this book, I'm always referring to green cardamom pods.) The seeds have a unique, warming flavor, with notes of lemon, pepper, and camphor. Once the seeds are ground they have a tendency to lose their flavor quickly, which is why it's best to leave the pods whole until ready to use. Cardamom is used to flavor both sweet and savory dishes alike, and in Damascus it's in the ground coffee you buy to make Turkish Coffee (page 139).

Citric Acid (*Hamud Lamoun*): Also called lemon salt or sour salt, citric acid is found naturally in citrus fruits. It has a sour taste and is often used as a preservative, or to give dishes a pleasant tart tang. It's handy to keep this in your pantry, as it can be substituted for fresh lemon juice in just about any recipe (the one exception I can think of is Lemony Mint Salad Dressing on page 28). To substitute, 1 large lemon = 3 to 4 tablespoons of fresh lemon juice = ¼ teaspoon citric acid. If you're using citric acid to replace lemon juice, keep in mind that you may need to add a bit of water as necessary to compensate for the lack of liquid.

Clarified Butter (*Ghee* or *Samneh*): Butter that has had the milk solids and water removed resulting in a higher smoke point, which makes it useful for cooking at higher temperatures. Because of its low water content, clarified butter is ideal for use in many rice dishes, as well as in cookies—particularly, Butter Cookies (page 123)—and other confections. Clarified butter can be easily made: melt unsalted butter over low heat and cook it until foam rises to the top. Remove from heat, skim the foam off the surface, and strain the liquid through a double-cheesecloth lined mesh sieve, discarding the solids. Store in an airtight container at cool room temperature or in the fridge.

Dried Limes (*Loomi*): Made from Persian limes that are dried until the insides turn black. They are about the size of golf balls or a little larger, and the outside color ranges from tan to brownish-black, but the darker variety is generally more flavorful. They taste sour, but without the brightness found in fresh limes, and have a complex, slightly fermented flavor. They are commonly used in dishes from the Arabian Gulf area, including Baked Chicken with Red Rice Pilaf (page 96) and Rice Pilaf with Spiced Smoked Chicken (page 94). If a recipe calls for grinding dried limes, do so right before you're ready to use them, as their flavor diminishes once ground.

Dates (*Tamar*): The fruit that grows on the date palm tree, *Phoenix dactylifera*. There are many different varieties of dates, which are divided into the following categories based on their sugar and moisture contents: soft (including Medjool), semi-dry (such as Deglet Noor), and dry (for example, Thoory). Dates undergo four different stages of ripening where they change color from green to yellow, orange, or red and then finally to brown; their texture also changes from crunchy to soft, and their flavor becomes sweet. Dates are thought of as a fairly healthy food, containing a wide range of vitamins and minerals, as well as fiber. Dates play an important role in Middle Eastern

Above: Dried Limes (Loomi)
Below: Persian Limes

cuisine. They contain simple sugars that help to quickly restore energy, which makes them the ideal food to break your fast with during the Islamic holy month of Ramadan. Dates are used as the filling for Date-Filled Cookies (page 118).

Fava Beans (*Foul*): Also called broad beans. They grow in slender green pods that are usually anywhere from 5 to 10 inches (12.75 to 25 cm) long and hold about three to eight beans, depending on their size. To remove fresh fava beans from the pod, either pull down on the stem so the pod opens, or cut a slit along one of the side of the pod. Before they can be eaten, the beans' outer skins must be removed. Do this by blanching the shelled beans for two minutes in boiling water and then plunge them into an ice

bath; the skins should slip right off. Once the outer skin is removed, fresh fava beans are delicious sautéed with a little olive oil, salt, pepper, garlic, and cilantro. Although they can be eaten fresh, they are commonly dried. Cooked fava beans are the main component in Mashed Fava Beans with Olive Oil, Lemon Juice, & Garlic (page 76) and are also frequently used to make Falafel (page 81).

Grape Leaves (*Waraq al Ainab or Dawali*): These are the tender leaves that grow on grapevines; they are used to make Vegetarian Stuffed Grape Leaves (page 71). If you have access to fresh grape leaves that have not been sprayed with pesticides, look for leaves that are the size of the palm of your hand or larger, that are free from holes or blem-

ishes. Before stuffing grape leaves, they require a little bit of preparation. Rinse them under cold running water, trim off the stems (without cutting the leaves), and blanch them for 2 to 3 minutes in a large pot of boiling water with 1 tablespoon salt and 1 teaspoon sugar. Rinse and drain them, and then they are ready to use or freeze (they can also be canned in a brine solution). To freeze, pat each leaf dry and then stack them on top of each other (try to place as many in a stack as you will need for a recipe); place the stack(s) in a plastic bag, press out all the air, and freeze. If you don't have access to fresh grape leaves, you can buy them frozen, canned, or jarred, just be sure to soak them for about 10 minutes in hot water (changing the water three times) before using.

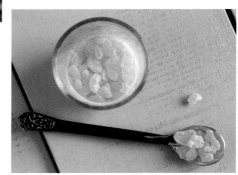

Mastic (*Miskeh*): A resin that comes from the mastic tree (*Pistacia lentiscus*) in eastern Mediterranean countries such as Turkey and Greece. To produce the resin, sap from the trees are dried into pale yellow or ivory colored "tears" that look like small pebbles of beach glass. Mastic is highly aromatic, with a strong licorice-like, piney flavor. Before being added to recipes, mastic should be ground, which is easiest to do by freezing it for 20 minutes, then grinding it in a mortar and pestle with a pinch of sugar (or salt, if the recipe is savory); don't use a spice grinder, as the mastic will gum it up. It is used sparingly in puddings like Lebanese Nights (page 121), and in addition to flavor, it lends a chewy texture to Rose and Pistachio Ice Cream (page 131).

Marrow Squash

Zucchini

Marrow Squash (*Kousa*): This is a type of summer squash similar to zucchini, but lighter in color and smaller and slightly more bulbous in size. It is commonly hollowed out and stuffed for Stuffed Marrow Squash (page 107) in Middle Eastern cooking. When choosing marrow squash to stuff, look for squash that is about 5 inches (12.75 cm) long and about 1½ to 2 inches (3.75 to 5 cm) in diameter at its thickest part. If you can't find marrow squash, zucchini can be used instead (see Hollowing Out Vegetables to Stuff, page 12).

It can also be chewed with a little wax as a sort of chewing gum.

Middle Eastern Cheese (*Jibneh*): There are many kinds of sheep, goat, and cow's milk cheeses native to the Middle East. Quite a few are salty and/or brined, and must be soaked in water to remove the excessive saltiness before being used in recipes. In the Middle East, cheese is commonly eaten with smaller meals (i.e., breakfast or dinner), along with tea to balance out the cheese's salty flavor. Perhaps the most well known Middle Eastern cheese is Halloumi, a salty, firm, brined cheese that squeaks when chewed. It has a high melting point, which makes it good for frying or grilling in recipes like Pan-Seared White Cheese (page 68). Ackawi, which comes from Acre, Palestine, is a salty, semi-firm, smooth cheese that melts similarly to mozzarella. After soaking in water to remove the salty flavor, this cheese becomes significantly softer; it is commonly used as table cheese. Nabulsi originated in Nablus, Palestine, and is a salty, semi-firm, brined cheese made by boiling Ackawi either with or without other spices and flavorings; nigella seeds are frequently used. Nabulsi is typically used to make Sweet Cheese Pastry (page 122). It can be used almost interchangeably with Halloumi in savory dishes. Shellal is a salty, stringy Syrian cheese that this made of cheese strands twisted together;

it also melts similarly to mozzarella. It is quite common to find Shellal with nigella seeds woven in with the cheese strands. Beladi is a soft, mildly tangy cheese that is typically made of goat milk; my favorite substitute for this cheese is farmer's cheese made from goat milk, if available. A recipe for Yogurt Cheese is found on page 73 and Spiced Cheese Balls is on page 69.

Mint (*Naa'na*): A bright-flavored herb commonly used in Middle Eastern cuisine. Both fresh and dried mint is used in various salad, soup, and sauce (particularly, yogurt-based sauces) recipes, and as garnishes. Mint is frequently steeped with tea and made into an elixir to drink after a large meal, as it is said to relieve indigestion.

Nigella Seeds (*Habbat al Barakeh*): Also called black seeds, their name literally translates to "the blessed seed." Nigella seeds are small and black, with a three dimensional, teardrop-like shape. They're related to buttercups, and they take their name from the lovely-named *Nigella sativa* plant that they come from. They are revered medicinally in Islam, and it is said that the Prophet Mohammed (peace be upon him) once stated that black seeds are "a remedy for all diseases except death." Nigella seeds have an interesting flavor—peppery, nutty, smoky, slightly bitter, and strangely, a little bit like oregano. They are a common addition to cheeses, breads, and pastries.

Orange Blossom Water (*Ma' al Zaher*): Also called orange flower water or just flower water, this clear liquid is distilled water made from orange blossoms. It is slightly bitter and very fragrant; to me, it smells like Damascus itself. It is used judiciously along with rose blossom water to flavor sweets and less frequently, savory dishes. It is the main flavoring in Scented Sugar Syrup (page 28) and White Coffee (page 139).

Persian Cucumber (*Khiear*): Small and slender cucumbers with very few seeds and a subtly sweet flavor. They are perfect for dicing up for salads or slicing up for maza platters. If you can't find them, you can use any other small cucumber you can find (such as Lebanese or Japanese); or use English cucumber instead (1 English cucumber equals approximately 3 to 4 Persian cucumbers).

Pine Nuts (*Snobar*): The edible seeds found beneath the scales of pinecones from certain varieties of pine trees. In Middle Eastern cuisine, longer, oval shaped pine nuts are preferred over the shorter, more round variety. Pine nuts are ivory colored with a soft, almost buttery texture and a nutty, mildly piney flavor. They are frequently toasted in a bit of clarified butter or olive oil and used as a garnish for rice dishes; they have a tendency to burn easily, so when toasting them, be sure to keep the heat low, stir frequently, and don't walk away from them. Due to their high oil content, it's best to store pine nuts in the freezer.

Pomegranate Molasses (*Dibis Rouman*): Pomegranate juice that has been reduced to thick brownish-reddish syrup. It has a very concentrated tangy, sweet/tart flavor and is frequently used in savory dishes, such as Bell Pepper Walnut Dip (page 72) and Meat and Vegetable Casserole with

Pomegranate (page 103). Also, spread a little on a falafel sandwich and you'll have everyone wondering about your delicious secret ingredient. If you can't find pomegranate molasses, you can easily make it by simmering 4 cups (1 liter) of pomegranate juice over medium heat until it's reduced to ½ cup (125 ml), then store in your refrigerator.

Purslane (*Baqli*): Also called lamb's lettuce, lamb's tongue, or mâché, the leaves of this leafy green vegetable look like little lamb's tongues and grow in clusters. Its extensive root system allows it to thrive in poor soils and dry conditions (it's because of this that purslane is often thought of as a weed by those who aren't familiar with it). Purslane is prized in Middle Eastern cuisine for its delicious, slightly nutty flavor with a hint of bitterness. It's a favorite ingredient in Herb Salad with Tangy Dressing and Croutons (page 48).

Roasted Green Wheat (*Freekeh*): This ancient grain is green wheat that is

harvested young, sun-dried, and then fire-roasted. It has a very unique nutty, smoky flavor that is delicious in dishes like Roasted Green Wheat with Chicken (page 89). When purchasing, look for coarsely cracked green wheat that smells deeply smoky and is greenish-brown in color.

Rose Water (*Ma' al Ward*): This clear liquid is distilled water made from rose petals. Similar to orange blossom water, it is slightly bitter and very fragrant. It is used sparingly, usually in conjunction with orange blossom water, to flavor sweets and sometimes savory dishes. Along with orange blossom water, it is the main flavoring in Rose and Orange Blossom-Scented Milk Pudding (page 127).

Saffron (*Zafaran*): This spice is the stigmas of the *Crocus sativus* flower; it can be found in whole threads or ground, but using whole threads is preferred. Saffron has a bittersweet, earthy flavor and should be used sparingly, as using too much may cause a dish to turn overly bitter or metallic. Saffron is deep red in color and gives a lovely golden hue to dishes such as Saffron Rice with Golden Raisins and Pine Nuts (page 61). Turmeric can be substituted to achieve a similar color; however, it will not yield the same flavor.

Semolina (*Smeed*): Coarse or fine-ground durum wheat. It is commonly used to make custard-like dishes, such as Lebanese Nights (page 121). It is also used to give a rustic texture to cakes (see Coconut Semolina Cake, page 130), and a crumbly, coarse texture to cookies.

Shredded Phyllo Dough (*Kataifi*): Phyllo dough that is shredded into thin, vermicelli-like strands. It gives a dish great texture, since it becomes crisp once cooked. In Middle Eastern cuisine, *kataifi* is commonly shaped into cigars, cones, cups, or nests, and used as the basis for sweets; it is also used to make Sweet Cheese Pastry (page 122). *Kataifi* is most commonly found frozen; once you're ready to use it, let it thaw in the fridge overnight and then let it come to room temperature for about an hour before working with it (keep it in its package while thawing so it doesn't dry out). If you're making *Knafeh bil Jiben* you don't have to take as much care with your *kataifi*, since it will be crushed anyway. However, if you want to shape the dough to make small sweets it should be handled similarly to phyllo dough so it doesn't dry out. When you're ready to use it, lay a piece of plastic wrap on a large baking sheet, then unwrap the *kataifi*, place it on the prepared sheet, and cover with another piece of plastic wrap. Then lay a towel that has been slightly dampened on top to help keep the dough chilled while you're working with it.

Sour Black Cherry Pits (*Mahlab*): A beautifully scented spice that is the dried kernel from sour black cherry pits. The whole kernels are small (about 5 mm long), tear-shaped, and tan colored, but mahlab is also commonly found ground. It smells of cherries and almonds and is slightly sweet, but with a pleasant, nutty bitterness. It gives a lovely flavor to breads, cakes, cookies, and pastries, and is found in Cake Spice Mix (page 29).

Sumac (*Sumac*): Not to be confused with poison sumac, this spice is the dried berry of non-poisonous sumac bushes. Depending on the variety used, sumac's color can range from brick red to purple to brown. It has a fruity, sour taste similar to lemon, and lends a bright flavor and lovely color to dishes like Roasted Chicken with Flatbread (page 97). It is also frequently used to flavor or garnish dips, such as Bell Pepper Walnut Dip (page 72), and is found in Thyme Spice Mix (page 29).

Tahini (*Tahina*): In Middle Eastern cooking, this refers to a beige-colored, thick and creamy paste of ground raw sesame seeds. Sesame seed paste, which is made from roasted sesame seeds, has a slightly different flavor but can be used as a substitute if tahini isn't available. Tahini has a nutty, slightly bitter flavor and is used frequently in both savory and sweet dishes, such as Hummus (page 79), Eggplant Dip (page 64), and Sesame Fudge (page 119). Tahini should be stored in the pantry until opened, but once opened, give it a stir (to equally distribute the oil) and keep it in the fridge for six months to a year.

Tamarind (*Tamar Hindi*): Literally meaning "Indian date," this fruit grows in curved brown pods on tamarind trees. These bushy trees are indigenous to tropical Africa but have also been cultivated in other tropical areas, including India. The pods' hard exterior turns brittle when the fruit is ripe, and it protects the seeds and fibrous, edible reddish-brown pulp inside. The pulp is pressed into a moist paste, which is how tamarind is commonly found in grocery stores. Tamarind has a very refreshing sweet/tart taste and is used to flavor savory sauces and make Tamarind Juice Drink (page 137).

Basic Recipes

Many recipes in this section are so basic that they cross cultural borders and can be used in different applications in any number of cuisines from around the world. Creamy Garlic Mayonnaise, one of the variations of Creamy Garlic Sauce (Toumieh) (below), which is an integral addition to Spiced Shawarma Chicken Wraps (Shawarma Dajaj) (page 92), can be used as you would use any other mayonnaise. Apple Vinegar (Khul Toofah) (page 26) not only has a whole host of applications, but is probably one of the tastiest vinegars you'll ever experience (more like a cross between apple cider and vinegar than anything else…it s so much sweeter than you'd expect). The Spice Mixes (Baharat) (page 29) are also an indispensible resource; I like to keep a jar of Seven Spice Mix (page 29) in my pantry at all times; for a quick way to add a huge flavor punch, nothing beats a sprinkle of this mix on red meat, poultry, or fish before cooking.

Creamy Garlic Sauce — TOUMIEH

Toumieh, which is commonly referred to as "Toum," is a very potent garlic sauce that is ubiquitous in Middle Eastern kitchens. Toum is a difficult sauce to make and master, since in its authentic state it is just an emulsification of garlic and lemon juice in oil, made with a mortar and pestle. If the sauce breaks and the oil separates there is no recovering it, but it is possible to save it with a thickener (although at this point the sauce is no longer pure Toumieh). This sauce can be used as the base for soups, sauces, salad dressings, or dips; or as its own condiment eaten with plain bread, in sandwiches, on rice, or with other finished dishes.

The variation I give for this recipe is basically just a garlic mayonnaise. The egg acts as a stabilizer, making this sauce much easier to master and faster to make than original Toumieh. Incidentally, this is the sauce that you will commonly find used in restaurants in the Middle East, particularly in foods like Spiced Shawarma Chicken Wraps. This sauce can be made using two egg whites or one whole egg; however, using a whole egg yields a much creamier, richer tasting sauce. If you're feeling adventurous, feel free to make the sauce the old-fashioned way with a mortar and pestle, otherwise, a blender works fine.

Yields *about 1 cup (225 g)*
Preparation Time: *10 minutes*

1 head garlic, (12-15 cloves) peeled
½ teaspoon salt
¾ cup (200 ml) oil
2 tablespoons lemon juice

Optional Thickeners
½ cup (110 g) Yogurt Cheese (Labneh) (page 73)

Or
½ cup (110 g) mayonnaise

1 Crush the garlic and salt in a mortar and pestle until it forms a smooth paste.
2 Add the oil, drop by drop, while mixing (after you've added 1 tablespoon of oil drop-by-drop, you can add the oil a little faster). Make sure the oil you add is fully incorporated before adding any more.
3 Once you've added ½ cup (125 ml) oil, alternate between adding the oil and lemon juice, and continue mixing until smooth and creamy.
4 At this point, if you want to thicken the garlic sauce, you can add the optional thickeners listed. If you choose to add a thickener, start by mixing in a little bit at a time and increase the amount until the sauce is as thick as you want it.

VARIATION
Garlic Mayonnaise

2 cloves garlic, crushed in a mortar and pestle with ½ teaspoon salt
2 large egg whites or 1 large egg
1 cup (250 ml) oil
1 tablespoon lemon juice
1 tablespoon cold water

1 Crush the garlic and salt in a mortar and pestle until it forms a smooth paste.
2 Whisk together the garlic paste and egg until well blended.
3 Add the oil, drop-by-drop, while whisking (after you've added 1 tablespoon of oil drop-by-drop, you can add the oil a little faster). Make sure the oil you add is fully incorporated before adding any more.
4 Once you've added ½ cup (125 ml) oil, alternate between gradually adding the oil and lemon juice and continue mixing until fully incorporated.
5 Add the cold water and mix until smooth and creamy.

Clotted Cream

ISHTA

Traditionally, *Ishta* is the cream that is skimmed off the top of whole milk as it cooks down; the cream thickens considerably as it cools and should be stored in the fridge. The process of cooking the milk and skimming of the *Ishta* as it forms takes quite a while, and while the end result is delicious, these days a healthier cream substitute (made of milk and cornstarch) is often used, this substitute is still called *Ishta* though!

This *Ishta* recipe can be used in Middle Eastern Pancakes (Qatayef) (page 124) or as an alternative filling instead of cheese for Sweet Cheese Pastry (page 122). If you want to serve *Ishta* as it is, you can give it a stir before chilling so it has a clotted-cream look to it, or you can leave it be without stirring before chilling so it can be unmolded like an Italian Panna Cotta. Either way is lovely, especially with a drizzle of Scented Sugar Syrup (page 28), Apple Vinegar (page 26), or honey, along with a sprinkle of chopped pistachios.

Serves *2 to 3*
Preparation Time: *2 minutes*
Cooking Time: *6 minutes, plus time for the cream to chill*

2 cups (500 ml) milk, divided
6 tablespoons corn starch
2 tablespoons sugar
½ teaspoon rose water (optional)
½ teaspoon orange blossom water (optional)

1 Whisk together ½ cup (125 ml) of milk with the cornstarch in a small bowl and set aside.
2 Combine the remaining 1½ cups (375 ml) milk and sugar in a medium-sized, heavy-bottomed saucepan over medium heat; cook until it comes to a boil, stirring occasionally. Whisk the cornstarch mixture into the boiling milk and cook 1 minute, whisking constantly.
3 Turn off the heat and stir in the rose water and orange blossom water, if using. Pour into individual serving dishes. Cool to room temperature, stir if you want a clotted cream look (don't stir if you want to unmold it), and then refrigerate until chilled, about 1 hour.

Sesame Sauce

TARATOOR

This sauce is a flavorful condiment for fried vegetables, falafel, shawarma, or fish. Both variations keep very well for up to 5 days if refrigerated.

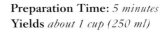

Preparation Time: *5 minutes*
Yields *about 1 cup (250 ml)*

½ cup (120 g) tahini
2 tablespoons fresh lemon juice
½ cup (125 ml) plus 2 tablespoons water
2 cloves garlic, crushed in a mortar and pestle with ½ teaspoon salt

1 Whisk together the tahini and lemon juice in a medium bowl (the sauce will thicken).
2 Whisk in the water drop-by-drop at first, and then in a thin drizzle (the sauce will thicken even more at first and then thin out).
3 Stir in the garlic and refrigerate until serving.

VARIATION
Sesame Parsley Dip

BAQDOUNISIYEH

This version is a bit thicker; it's commonly scooped up with flatbread and eaten as a dip, but it also makes a fantastic dressing for salads or fried vegetables.

½ cup (120 g) tahini
2 tablespoons fresh lemon juice
½ cup (125 ml) water
2 cloves garlic, crushed in a mortar and pestle with ½ teaspoon salt
½ of a bunch of fresh parsley leaves, minced

1 Whisk together the tahini and lemon juice in a medium bowl (the sauce will thicken).
2 Whisk in the water drop-by-drop at first, and then in a thin drizzle (the sauce will thicken even more at first and then thin out).
3 Stir in the garlic and parsley and refrigerate until serving (it will thicken more as it sits).

Apple Vinegar
KHUL TOOFAH

When you're making something with apples that requires peeling them, like Apple Preserves (page 126), this recipe is the perfect use for the leftover peels. Similar to commercial raw, unfiltered apple cider vinegar, this vinegar is murky and brownish with sediment at the bottom. However, its flavor is sweeter and much more palatable than commercial vinegar and it is a real treat in salad dressings.

Yields *3 to 4 pints (1.5 to 2 liters)*
Preparation Time: *30 minutes, plus 2 to 6 months to ferment*

4 cups (1 liter) warm water
1 cup (250 g) sugar
Apple skins and cores from 2 lb (1 kg) apples
    (about 3 cups, slightly pressed down)
1 apple, grated (including skin and core)
Two thin pieces fresh ginger, (optional)
1 teaspoon oil

1 Sterilize a 2-liter (2.11 qts) canning jar.
2 Combine the water and sugar in a large measuring cup with a pour spout; stir until the sugar is completely dissolved and then cool to room temperature.
3 Add the apple skins, cores, and grated apple to the sterile jar along with the ginger, if using. Pour in the sugar water.
4 Cover the jar and leave it to form vinegar, opening it to stir once every day and make sure the apple skins are completely submerged; you can add more apple skins/cores during this time if you want. (This process can take anywhere from 2 to 6 months, depending on the weather. The vinegar is done fermenting when a white skin forms on top).
5 Strain the vinegar through a cheesecloth-lined sieve, wringing out the cheesecloth to extract as much liquid as possible.
6 To store, pour the vinegar into a glass bottle along with the oil; store at room temperature.

VARIATION
Grape Vinegar
KHUL AINAB

Use 3 cups (450 to 500 g) of de-stemmed grapes (any kind you like) instead of apple skins, cores, and the grated apple; proceed with the rest of the recipe.

Basic Savory Flat Pie Dough
AJEEN FATAYER

Ajeen Fatayer, the basic dough used to make a variety of savory pies, is a true Middle Eastern staple. To this day there are communal ovens in Damascus, a tradition that dates back to a time when very few homes had ovens of their own. Each family brought the filling of their choice to the baker at the communal oven, who used his own dough to make pies out of the filling provided. The family paid for the dough that the baker used and went home with the finished pies. This tradition has endured despite the fact that most Damascene homes now have their own oven.

Yields *This recipe makes enough dough to make one of the following recipes: Spiced Meat Flat Pies (page 35) Spinach Turnovers (page 36), or Thyme-Spiced Flat Pies (page 37).*
Preparation Time: *15 minutes, plus 1½ hours to let the dough rise*
Cooking Time: *See individual recipes*

3½ tablespoons olive oil, divided
2 teaspoons instant yeast
1½ teaspoons sugar
4 tablespoons warm water
3 cups (375 g) all-purpose flour, plus more for kneading
1¼ teaspoons fine salt
¾ cup (185 ml) milk, at room temperature

1 Brush ½ tablespoon of oil on the inside of a large bowl and set aside.
2 Mix together the yeast, sugar, and warm water in a small bowl until the sugar is dissolved.
3 Whisk together the flour and salt in a large bowl. Use a wooden spoon to stir the yeast mixture into the dry ingredients, and then stir in the remaining 3 tablespoons of oil. Gradually stir in enough milk to form "shaggy" dough (you may not need all the milk).
4 Turn the dough out onto a lightly floured surface and knead about 5 minutes; the dough is done being kneaded when you press a finger into it and the indentation remains.
5 Transfer the dough to the oiled bowl and roll it gently to coat with oil. Cover the bowl with a slightly damp towel and let sit until doubled in size, about 1½ hours.
6 Use the dough to make savory pies, such as Spinach Turnovers (page 36), Thyme-Spiced Flat Pies (page 37), or Spiced Meat Flat Pies (page 35).

Pickles

MEKHALLEL

These pickles are made through lactic acid fermentation (also called lacto fermentation), a pickling process that has been used for centuries across the world (German sauerkraut, Korean kimchi, and Mexican curtido are all made this way). Through this process, harmless bacteria are allowed to proliferate, causing the natural sugars in food to be used as cellular energy for the bacteria, thus creating the by-product lactic acid. Lactic acid not only preserves food (i.e., turns it into pickles), but also increases vitamin content, makes food more digestible, and provides a natural source of healthy probiotics.

These pickles also taste pretty delicious, and are often found on maza platters or in Spiced Shawarma Chicken Wraps (page 92).

If you prefer a crunchier pickle, add one to two small, clean fresh grape leaves.

Yields *1 liter (1.06 qt) jar of pickles*
Preparation Time: *10 minutes, plus up to 20 days for the pickles to ferment*

1 cup (250 ml) hot water
2 tablespoons salt
2 teaspoons sugar
7-10 Persian or Japanese cucumbers washed and ends slightly trimmed
2 cloves garlic, peeled
Purified water, to cover the cucumber
½ teaspoon oil

1 Combine the 1 cup (250 ml) hot water, salt, and sugar in a large measuring cup with a pour spout; stir until the salt and sugar are completely dissolved and then cool to room temperature.
2 Sterilize a 1-liter (1.06 qt) canning jar.
3 Cut the cucumbers into spears by cutting them in half lengthwise, and then cutting each half lengthwise into 3 equal pieces.
4 Put 1 clove of garlic in the bottom of the jar, add the cucumber spears, and then add the other clove of garlic on top.
5 Pour in the water/salt/sugar mixture, then add enough purified water so that the cucumbers are completely covered, leaving about 1 inch (2.5 cm) of free space at the top.
6 Let the jar sit at room temperature to form pickles. The pickles are ready to eat when the cucumber turns khaki green in color, and they smell faintly of vinegar. This will take about 5 to 7 days in hot weather and 15 to 20 days in colder weather.
7 Once the pickles are ready to eat, drizzle in the oil and store refrigerated.

Lemony Mint Salad Dressing

This dressing is used to dress most Middle Eastern salads, including Middle Eastern Salad (page 47), Colorful Cabbage Salad with Lemony Salad Dressing (page 40), Roasted Eggplant Salad (page 44), and Vibrant Beet Salad (page 43).

Yields *a little over ½ cup (125 ml)*
Preparation Time: *2 minutes*

1 clove garlic, crushed in a mortar and pestle with ¼ teaspoon salt
Juice of 1 lemon (about 3 tablespoons)
½ cup (125 ml) olive oil
1 tablespoon minced fresh mint leaves

Whisk together the garlic/salt mixture and lemon juice; gradually whisk in the olive oil in a thin drizzle. Stir in the mint, if using.

VARIATION
Olive Oil Vinaigrette

Use 2 tablespoons of Apple Vinegar (page 26), or any vinegar you like, instead of the lemon juice; proceed with the recipe.

Scented Sugar Syrup QATER

This syrup can be made either thin or thick; unless specified in a particular recipe, assume it refers to thin syrup. *Qater* should generally be cooled before using, since this allows the syrup to thicken. Also, when it's used to sweeten a cake, such as Sweet Cheese Pastry (page 122) or Coconut Semolina Cake (page 130), the cake should be hot and the syrup should be cool so that the cake fully absorbs it.

Yields *about 1 cup (250 ml) of thin syrup or ²/₃ cup (160 ml) of thick syrup*
Preparation Time: *1 minute*
Cooking Time: *10 minutes*

1 cup (225 g) sugar
½ cup (125 ml) water
½ tablespoon fresh lemon juice
½ tablespoon rose water or orange blossom water

1 Add the sugar, water and lemon juice to a medium, thick-bottomed saucepan, and bring to a boil over medium heat, giving the pan an occasional swirl and skimming off any foam on the surface.
2 Turn heat down slightly and boil 2 minutes (if you want thin syrup) and up to 5 minutes (if you want thick syrup), swirling the pan occasionally. (The syrup will thicken more upon cooling.)
3 Turn off heat and stir in the rose water or orange blossom water; cool to room temperature, then use.

Left Top : Lemony mint salad dressing
Left Bottom: Olive oil

Lamb and Rice Stuffing

Beef can be used instead of lamb in this stuffing. This recipe yields enough stuffing to make 1 batch of Stuffed Marrow Squash (page 107), or to stuff 2 lb/1 kg of baby eggplant, small bell peppers, or cabbage.

Preparation Time: *15 minutes*
Cooking Time: *7 minutes*

1 cup (215 g) medium-grain white rice, rinsed
2 tablespoons oil
2 onions, finely diced
1¼ teaspoons salt
3 cloves garlic, crushed in a mortar and pestle
¾ teaspoon Syrian Spice Mix (page 29)
½ teaspoon cumin
½ teaspoon ground coriander
⅛ teaspoon freshly ground black pepper
½ lb (250 g) ground lamb or beef
3 tablespoons butter, melted

1 Soak the rice in tepid water for 10 minutes; drain.
2 Heat the oil in a large skillet over medium heat; add the onion and salt and cook until softened, about 5 to 7 minutes, stirring occasionally. Add the garlic, Syrian Spice Mix, cumin, ground coriander, and black pepper, and sauté 1 minute more, stirring constantly. Let cool.
3 Use your hands to mix together the drained rice, onion mixture, raw meat, and melted butter in a large bowl.

VARIATION
Meat Stuffing for Stuffed Grape Leaves

Increase rice to 2 cups (430 g), increase oil to 4 tablespoons and add ¾ teaspoon turmeric when you add the other spices; proceed with the rest of the recipe as written.

Basic Spice Mixes BAHARAT

Here are a few basic spice mixes used in Middle Eastern cooking. You may be able to find some of the mixes available commercially at Middle Eastern grocery stores, but others may be hard to locate and you'll need to make your own. Additionally, making your own spice mix lets you customize it to suit your tastes. (Typically, spice mixes vary from region to region and even family to family, so feel free to play with the components and measurements if you like.) Thyme Spice Mix is perhaps the most commonly known Middle Eastern spice mix. It can be used in any number of recipes, such as Thyme-Spiced Flat Pies (page 37) or Spiced Cheese Balls (page 69), but it is commonly served with olive oil and flatbread. To eat this dish (which is called *Za'atar wa Zayt*), a piece of flatbread is torn off, dipped in a dish of olive oil, and then dipped in a dish of *Za'atar*. This is a common breakfast dish, as the herbs in *Za'atar* are thought to improve memory and concentration; my husband remembers his grade school teacher in Syria telling his class to always eat *Za'atar wa Zayt* for breakfast, especially before an exam.

Mendy Spice Mix
3 bay leaves
3 dried limes (loomi)
One 3 in (7.5 cm) cinnamon stick, broken in half
1½ tablespoons whole green cardamom pods
1 tablespoon whole cloves
½ tablespoon whole black peppercorns
1 whole nutmeg
One 1 in (25 mm) piece dried galangal (blue ginger) or ginger

Syrian Spice Mix
½ tablespoon ground cinnamon
1¼ teaspoons ground allspice
½ teaspoon ground nutmeg
¼ teaspoon ground cloves

Kebseh Spice Mix
½ tablespoon ground cumin
½ tablespoon ground coriander 1 teaspoon ground red pepper (cayenne)
1 pinch saffron threads or ⅛ teaspoon ground turmeric
1 batch Mendy Spice Mix

Meat Spice Mix
2 teaspoons ground turmeric
1 batch Nine Spice Mix

Chicken Spice Mix
½ teaspoon ground fennel
¼ teaspoon ground anise
1 batch Meat Spice Mix

Thyme Spice Mix
1½ tablespoons ground sumac
1½ tablespoons sesame seeds, toasted
1½ tablespoons dried thyme leaves
½ tablespoon ground thyme
2 teaspoons dried crushed oregano
2 teaspoons dried crushed savory (optional)
1 teaspoon ground marjoram
1 teaspoon coarse salt

Cake Spice Mix
½ teaspoon ground mahlab (Sour Black Cherry Pits, see page 23)
¼ teaspoon ground ginger
¼ teaspoon ground fennel
¼ teaspoon ground anise
1 batch Syrian Spice Mix

Four Spice Mix
1 tablespoon ground black pepper
1 tablespoon ground allspice
1 teaspoon ground cinnamon
½ teaspoon ground nutmeg

Nine Spice Mix
1 teaspoon ground cloves
½ teaspoon ground cardamom
1 batch Seven Spice Mix

Seven Spice Mix
2 teaspoons ground sweet paprika
1½ teaspoons ground coriander
1½ teaspoons ground cumin
1 batch Four Spice Mix

1 For each mix, combine all spices in a small bowl.
2 If the mix has whole spices (such as the Mendy Spice Mix and Kebseh Spice Mix), grind them in a spice grinder and strain through a fine mesh sieve, if desired.
3 Store in an airtight container at room temperature.

Spinach Turnovers
(page 36)

CHAPTER ONE

Breads and Pies

Bread in the Middle East is found at just about every meal (the one exception I've noticed is for meals containing a rice dish). Bread is typically passed around the table and used as a utensil for eating food from a common dish (no forks/spoons/knives necessary!). The bread itself is always incredibly fresh, as in it was made that morning (stale bread has other uses; see Herb Salad with Tangy Dressing and Croutons (Fattoush) on page 48 and Creamy Chickpea and Yogurt Casserole (Tissiyeh or Fetteh bil Hummous) on page 80. The most common kind of bread eaten is flatbread, like Middle Eastern Flatbread (Khubz Arabi) on page 32, which is disc shaped and hollow inside like a pita. It is usually not as thick and chewy as pita bread though; since it's eaten with most meals, it should be fresh and delicious but not filling, or you wouldn't be able to eat anything else!

Middle Eastern Flatbreads

KHUBZ ARABI

This is the kind of bread that is present at just about every meal in the Middle East; forks and spoons may or may not be there, since this bread acts as both. Most meals are eaten family-style, with the food placed around the table (or on top of a newspaper-lined floor); this bread is then passed around and everyone digs in. This bread has a large pocket inside; this is because while cooking, steam causes the dough to puff up, and later when the bread is removed from the oven it cools and deflates, leaving a pocket. The trick to this is using a very hot oven. Like any bread, this is best eaten fresh the same day it's made; however, if you let some get stale you can use it to make Herb Salad with Tangy Dressing and Croutons (page 48) or Creamy Chickpea and Yogurt Casserole (page 80).

Preparation Time: *35 minutes, plus about 2 hours to let the dough rise*
Cooking Time: *25 minutes*
Yields *10 large flatbreads*

4½ tablespoons olive oil, divided

2 teaspoons instant yeast

1 tablespoon sugar

4 tablespoons warm water

5 cups (650 g) all-purpose flour,
    plus more for kneading

2 teaspoons fine salt

1 cup (250 ml) plus 2 tablespoons milk, room temperature

1 Brush ½ tablespoon of oil on the inside of a large bowl and set aside.
2 Mix together the yeast, sugar, and warm water in a small bowl until the sugar is dissolved.
3 Whisk together the flour and salt in a large bowl. Use a wooden spoon to stir the yeast mixture into the dry ingredients, then stir in the remaining 4 tablespoons of oil. Stir in the milk.
4 Turn the dough out onto a lightly floured surface and knead for about 5 minutes; the dough is done being kneaded when you press a finger into it and the indentation remains.
5 Transfer the dough to the oiled bowl and roll it gently to coat with oil. Cover the bowl with a slightly damp towel and let it sit until it's doubled in size, about 1½ hours.
6 Gently deflate the dough, shape it back into a ball, and place it back into the bowl. Cover the bowl with a slightly damp towel and let sit until puffed, about 30 minutes.
7 Preheat the oven (from the lower heating elements) to 500°F (260°C) and position a rack in the lower ⅓ of the oven. Place a large baking sheet or a clay baking stone on the rack.
8 Divide the dough into 10 equal pieces and shape each into a ball. Place all the dough except 1 piece back into the bowl and cover with the towel. Lightly flour your work surface and, with a rolling pin, roll 1 piece of dough out to a circle about 10 to 12 inches (25 to 30 cm) in diameter.
9 Transfer the rolled out dough to the preheated baking sheet or clay baking stone. Cook until it's puffed and there are a few light golden spots on the bottom, about 2 to 3 minutes. Transfer the bread to a cloth or paper-lined surface to cool completely.
10 Roll out the rest of the dough, and bake and cool it the same way. Wrap the cooled bread in a soft cloth or zip-top plastic bag to stay fresh.

Sesame Seed Breads

KHUBZ BIL SIMSEM

I first had this bread with my husband at our favorite restaurant in Amman. Its tender crumb and chewy exterior make for a perfect loaf, not to mention that the sesame seeds add a deliciously subtle nutty flavor. It was literally all I could do not to fill up on this bread (along with olive oil, olives, and cheese) before dinner. Instead of sesame seeds, you can use nigella seeds (page 21) to sprinkle on top if you like.

Preparation Time: *20 minutes, plus about 1 hour, 45 minutes for the dough to rise*
Cooking Time: *50 minutes*
Yields *6 loaves*

2 tablespoons plus 2 teaspoons olive oil, divided
2 teaspoons instant yeast
1½ teaspoons sugar
2 tablespoons warm water
3½ cups (500 g) all-purpose flour, plus more
  for kneading
1 teaspoon salt
1 cup (250 ml) warm milk
2 teaspoons black or white sesame seeds
  (or a mix of both)

1 Brush 2 teaspoons oil on the inside of a large bowl and set aside.
2 Mix together the yeast, sugar, and warm water in a small bowl until the sugar is dissolved.
3 Combine the flour and salt in a large bowl. Whisk together 1 cup (250 ml) of warm water and the powdered milk in a small bowl; measure out 1 tablespoon and transfer it to a separate bowl to brush on the dough right before baking.
4 Stir the yeast mixture into the dry ingredients, then stir in the remaining 2 tablespoons of oil. Gradually stir in the water/powdered milk mixture to form a ball (you might need a little more liquid to get the dough to come together; if so, add warm water 1 teaspoon at a time).
5 Turn the dough out onto a lightly floured surface and knead for a couple of minutes; the dough is done being kneaded when you can press a finger into it and the indentation remains.
6 Transfer the dough to the oiled bowl and roll it gently to coat it with oil; cover the bowl with a towel and let it sit until it's doubled in size (about 1½ hours). Divide the dough into 6 equal pieces, and roll into oval-shaped loaves, about 6 inches (15 cm) long and 3 inches (7.5 cm) wide.
7 Preheat the oven to 400°F (200°C). Line 3 large baking sheets with parchment paper (if you don't have 3 large baking sheets, line up 3 pieces of parchment paper on the tabletop and transfer them to baking sheets as the sheets become available).
8 Transfer the loaves to the prepared baking sheets (2 loaves per sheet) and lightly brush them with the reserved milk; sprinkle on the sesame seeds. Let them rest until they start to puff up, about 10 to 15 minutes.
9 Bake the loaves 1 sheet at a time until light golden brown, about 16 minutes. Cool on a wire rack.

Spiced Meat Flat Pies

SFEEHA

This is another dish that varies greatly from family to family, even in the same area. Some prefer a short, crisp dough (that's more like a pastry crust) and others like it on a leavened, bread-y dough. Some add pomegranate molasses or sumac for a refreshing tangy flavor, and others leave it out. This is my mother-in-law's version, which I think is masterpiece. (Note: If you can find them, decorating the tops of these pies with pomegranate arils is a fun play on the pomegranate molasses that's in the recipe.)

The yogurt used in this recipe should be somewhat thick, but not as thick as Yogurt Cheese (page 73); you can use Greek-style yogurt or drain regular yogurt for a while in a cheesecloth-lined sieve.

Preparation Time: *1 hour, 15 minutes*
Cooking Time: *30 minutes*
Yields *16 pies*

1 batch Basic Savory Flat Pie Dough (page 26)
1 large onion
¾ lb (350 g) lean ground lamb or beef
2 tablespoons pomegranate molasses
6 tablespoons plain yogurt
2 tablespoons pine nuts
¾ teaspoon Meat Spice Mix (page 29)
¾ teaspoon salt
⅛ teaspoon freshly ground black pepper
Oil for the baking sheets and countertop
Plain yogurt (optional, for serving)
Fresh pomegranate seeds, to garnish (optional)

1 Prepare Basic Savory Flat Pie Dough and Meat Spice Mix.
2 Finely dice the onion, then transfer it to the bowl of a food processor and pulse a few times until it's very finely minced but not puréed. Combine the onion, raw meat, pomegranate molasses, yogurt, pine nuts, Meat Spice Mix, salt, and black pepper in a large bowl. Refrigerate 30 minutes and then pour off any liquid that has accumulated in the bottom of the bowl.
3 Preheat oven to 400°F (200°C) and lightly brush 2 large baking sheets with oil (alternatively, you can line them with parchment paper or silpat liners).
4 Gently deflate the dough, then divide into 16 equal pieces and shape the pieces into balls; put the balls back into the bowl, cover the bowl with a slightly damp towel, and let sit 5 to 10 minutes. Lightly brush olive oil onto your countertop (or whatever surface you want to use to press out the dough).
5 Work with 1 piece of dough at a time and use your hands to press it out on your oiled surface to a circle about 4 inches (10 cm) in diameter. Line up the pies about 2 inches (5 cm) apart on the oiled baking sheets; scoop 3 tablespoons of the meat mixture onto each pie and spread it in an even layer, leaving a ¼-inch (6 mm) rim around the outside of the pie.
6 Bake until puffed and golden brown on the edges, about 12 to 16 minutes, rotating the baking sheets once halfway through cooking.
7 Serve warm or at room temperature, alongside plain yogurt if desired.

VARIATION
Spiced Meat Flat Pies with Tomato

Omit the yogurt and pine nuts from the meat mixture; instead add ¾ lb (350 g) finely diced, de-seeded tomatoes and ½ teaspoon dried red pepper flakes (if desired). Proceed with the rest of the recipe as written.

⚘Spinach Turnovers⚘

FATAYER BIL SABANEKH

Spinach Turnovers is one of the many recipes that can be made with Basic Savory Flat Pie Dough (page 26). A combination of sumac and lemon juice gives these pastries a pleasant tang, and it's common to see a bowl of fresh lemon wedges served alongside for squeezing into the turnovers for people who like them even tangier. In the Middle East, spinach turnovers are served with a healthy amount of plain yogurt to round out the meal.

If you run out of filling but have leftover dough then you can make Thyme-Spiced Flat Pies (page 37) or shape the dough scraps into any shape you like and bake them along with the turnovers.

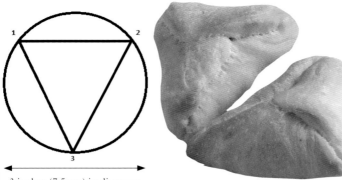

3 inches (7.5 cm) in diameter

1 batch Basic Savory Flat Pie Dough (page 26)
1 tablespoon olive oil
1 tablespoon canola oil, plus more as
   necessary for the spinach
1 large onion, finely diced
1 tablespoon sumac
1 lb (500 g) spinach
2 tablespoons fresh lemon juice
¾ teaspoon salt
½ teaspoon ground coriander
½ teaspoon cumin
⅛ teaspoon freshly ground black pepper
Olive oil to oil the baking sheets, countertop,
and tops of the turnovers
Fresh lemon wedges (optional, for serving)

Preparation Time: *1 hour, 30 minutes*
Cooking Time: *40 minutes*
Yields about *25 to 35 turnovers*

1 Prepare Basic Savory Flat Pie Dough.
2 Heat both the oils in a large skillet over medium heat; add the onion and sauté until softened but not browned, about 5 to 7 minutes, stirring occasionally. Remove from the heat and stir in the sumac.
3 Chop the spinach and remove any large stems; add it to a large pot with 2 cups (500 ml) of water. Cover the pot and cook over high heat until just wilted, about 8 to 10 minutes, stirring occasionally. Drain in a cheesecloth-lined colander and let it sit until the spinach is cool enough to handle, and then wring the cheesecloth to remove the excess water.
4 Combine the onion/sumac mixture, drained spinach, lemon juice, salt, coriander, cumin, and black pepper in a large bowl. The spinach should look slightly glossy, if it doesn't, stir in more canola oil, 1 teaspoon at a time, until it does. Be careful not to add too much. Taste the spinach; it should taste like a well-seasoned salad—if it doesn't, adjust seasonings (such as lemon juice, salt, pepper, and other spices) accordingly.
5 Preheat oven to 400°F (200°C) and lightly brush 2 large baking sheets with olive oil (alternatively, you can line them with parchment paper or silpat liners).
6 Gently deflate the dough, then divide into 2 equal pieces and shape the pieces into balls; put the balls back into the bowl, cover the bowl with a slightly damp towel, and let sit 5 to 10 minutes. Lightly brush olive oil onto your countertop (or whatever surface you want to use to roll out the dough).
7 Work with 1 piece of dough at a time and use your hands to gently stretch it out, then use a rolling pin to roll it out to a circle about 12 inches (30 cm) in diameter. Stamp out circles 3 inches (7.5 cm) in diameter with a round cookie cutter. Scoop about ½ tablespoon of spinach filling onto the center of each piece of dough. Repeat this process with the three remaining balls of dough. Gather the dough scraps into a ball, roll it out, and fill (only re-roll the scraps once to prevent the dough from toughening).
8 To form the turnovers, fold the dough along line 1-2 up and over onto the center, then do the same for the dough along line 2-3, and finally for line 1-3; pinch the dough together at the seams to seal it. (Alternatively, you can shape them into little pyramids: pull up lines 1-3 and 2-3 and pinch them together to form a seam, then pull up line 1-2 and pinch it together along the sides of the seam you just made to form the two remaining sides.)
9 Line up the turnovers (seam side up) about 2 inches (5 cm) apart on the prepared baking sheets and brush a little oil on top of each. Bake until golden brown, about 15 to 20 minutes, rotating the baking sheets once halfway through cooking. Serve hot, warm, or at room temperature.

Thyme Spiced Flat Pies

MANAQEESH

In the Middle East, children are encouraged to eat these pies for breakfast, since the herbs in Thyme Spice Mix supposedly help improve memory and concentration.

Preparation Time: *40 minutes*
Cooking Time: *30 minutes*
Yields *16 pies*

1 batch Basic Savory Flat Pie Dough (page 26)
1 batch plus 2 tablespoons Thyme Spice Mix (page 29)
3½ tablespoons olive oil
Olive oil for the baking sheets and countertop
Plain yogurt (optional, for serving)

1 Prepare Basic Savory Flat Pie Dough and Thyme Spice Mix.
2 Preheat oven to 400°F (200°C) and lightly brush 2 large baking sheets with olive oil (alternatively, you can line them with parchment paper or silpat liners). Mix the Thyme Spice Mix and 3½ tablespoons olive oil together in a small bowl and set aside.
3 Gently deflate the dough, then divide into 16 equal pieces and shape the pieces into balls; put the balls back into the bowl, cover the bowl with a slightly damp towel, and let sit 5 to 10 minutes. Lightly brush olive oil onto your countertop (or whatever surface you want to use to press out the dough).
4 Work with 1 piece of dough at a time and use your hands to press it out on your oiled surface to a circle about 3 to 4 inches (7.5 to 10 cm) in diameter. Line up the pies about 2 inches (5 cm) apart on the oiled baking sheets and spread about 1 teaspoon of the Thyme Spice Mix/olive oil onto each pie.
5 Bake until puffed and golden brown on the edges, about 12 to 14 minutes, rotating the baking sheets once halfway through cooking.
6 Serve at room temperature, alongside plain yogurt if desired.

Middle Eastern Salad (page 47)

CHAPTER TWO

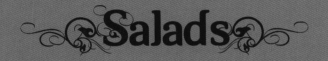
Salads

A Middle Eastern main meal isn't complete without a salad being present. Most of the time it is a basic salad of chopped vegetables that are dressed very simply with olive oil and lemon juice or vinegar (see Middle Eastern Salad (Salata) on page 47), but some meals call for a special salad. For example, Fish Pilaf with Caramelized Onion (Sayadieh bil Samek) (page 86) is frequently paired with Chopped Salad with Sesame Dressing (Salatit Tahina) (page 47), since tahini goes so nicely with fish, and Upside Down Rice Casserole (Maqluba) (page 114) is often served with Cucumber Yogurt Salad (Laban bil Khiear) (page 43), which not only adds great flavor to the steaming hot rice, but also helps cool it down. Other salads are useful for using up leftovers, such as stale bread used in Herb Salad with Tangy Dressing and Croutons (Fattoush) (page 48) Chickpeas leftover from making Falafel (Felafil) (page 81) or Hummus (Hummous bil Tahina or M'sebaha) (page 79) can be used in Chickpea Salad with Lemony Mint Salad Dressing (Salatit Hommous) (page 40).

Chickpea Salad with Lemony Mint Salad Dressing

SALATIT HOMMOUS

This is a rustic bean salad that's brightened with the flavor of parsley, lemon, and garlic. The mint adds a refreshing touch without being overpowering; if you don't have fresh mint on hand, you can use a teaspoon or so of crushed, dried mint. Canned chickpeas work just fine here, but if you have the time, you can cook up a batch of dried chickpeas to use (see Cooking Dried Beans and Lentils, page 11).

Serves *4 to 6*
Preparation Time: *5 minutes*

1 batch Lemony Mint Salad Dressing (page 28)
Two (15 oz) cans chickpeas, rinsed and drained
½ bunch fresh parsley leaves, minced
2 sprigs fresh mint leaves, minced
Freshly ground black pepper, to taste

1 Prepare Lemony Mint Salad Dressing.
2 Combine the dressing, chickpeas, parsley, and mint leaves in a large bowl; season with pepper.
3 Chill until ready to serve.

Colorful Cabbage Salad with Lemony Mint Salad Dressing

SALATIT MALFOOF

Cabbage makes this salad hearty and filling; also, it makes this salad a bit sturdier, as cabbage tends not to wilt as fast as lettuce-based salads.

Serves *6*
Preparation Time: *15 minutes*

1 batch Lemony Mint Salad Dressing (page 28)
½ small head Savoy or green cabbage (about ½ lb/250 g), halved, core removed, and chopped into thin shreds
½ small head red cabbage (about ½ lb/250 g), halved, core removed, and chopped into thin shreds
3 tomatoes, diced
4 green onions (scallions), white and green parts thinly sliced
3 sprigs fresh mint, minced
½ teaspoon salt
⅛ teaspoon freshly ground black pepper

1 Prepare Lemony Mint Salad Dressing.
2 Combine all ingredients in a large bowl.
3 Serve immediately.

Vibrant Beet Salad

SALATIT SHAMANDER BIL TAHINA

Beets are so naturally sweet that they're perfectly accentuated by a tangy Lemony Mint Salad Dressing.

Serves *4*
Preparation Time: *8 minutes*
Cooking Time: *25 minutes*

1 lb (500 g) fresh beets, stems trimmed
1 small onion, thinly sliced
½ bunch of fresh parsley, minced
½ batch Lemony Mint Salad Dressing (page 28)
Salt, to taste

1 Prepare Lemony Mint Salad Dressing.
2 Put the beet in a medium saucepan and add enough cold water to cover by about 1 to 2 inches (2.5 to 5 cm). Cover the saucepan, bring to a boil over high heat, and then turn the heat down and cook until tender (a paring knife should slide right in and out), about 20 to 30 minutes; drain the beets and transfer them to a bowl of ice water to cool.
3 Peel the beet (the skin should easily peel right off if you rub it), and then dice.
4 Toss the beet with all remaining ingredients and season with salt; chill until serving.

VARIATION
Beet Salad with Tahini Dressing

1 lb (500 g) fresh beets, stems trimmed
½ batch Sesame Sauce (page 25)
Salt, to taste

1 Prepare the Sesame Sauce.
2 Put the beet in a medium saucepan and add enough cold water to cover by about 1 to 2 inches (2.5 to 5 cm). Cover the saucepan, bring to a boil over high heat, and then turn the heat down and simmer until tender (a paring knife should slide right in and out), about 20 to 30 minutes; drain the beets and transfer them to a bowl of ice water to cool.
3 Peel the beet (the skin should easily peel right off if you rub it), and then dice.
4 Toss the beet with the Sesame Sauce and season with salt; chill until serving.

Cucumber Yogurt Salad

LABAN BIL KHIEAR

This salad is commonly used as a condiment for rice dishes, such as Upside-Down Rice Casserole (page 114). It's spooned on top of hot rice cooling it down, and adding a nice creamy tang.

Serves *4 to 6*
Preparation Time: *10 minutes*

2 Persian or Japanese cucumbers (or ½ of a regular cucumber), finely diced
2 cloves garlic, crushed in a mortar and pestle with ¼ teaspoon salt
2 cups (500 ml) plain yogurt
1 tablespoon lemon juice
¼ bunch fresh mint leaves, minced (or 2 teaspoons dried crushed mint)
1 tablespoon olive oil (optional)
Salt, to taste

1 Stir together all ingredients; season with additional salt as desired.
2 Refrigerate until serving.

Roasted Eggplant Salad

SALATIT BATINJAN

Since it's roasted, the flavor of eggplant in this salad is very mellow; if you prefer, the eggplant can be grilled for a nice smoky flavor. The sweetness of the tomato and the tart lemon dressing balance the flavors nicely.

Serves *4*
Preparation Time: *10 minutes, plus 15 minutes for the eggplant to cool*
Cooking Time: *40 minutes*

1 medium globe eggplant (¾ lb/350 g) globe eggplant
½ batch Lemony Mint Salad Dressing (page 28)
1 large tomato, diced
½ green bell pepper, deseeded and diced
1 small onion, minced
½ bunch fresh parsley leaves, minced with a couple of
    leaves reserved for garnish
Salt and freshly ground black pepper, to taste

1 Prepare Lemony Mint Salad Dressing.
2 Preheat oven to 400°F (200°C). Pierce the eggplant a few times with a sharp knife, transfer to a sheet pan, and roast until soft, about 40 minutes. (Alternatively, the whole eggplant can be grilled until tender.) When it's cool enough to handle, cut the eggplant in half lengthwise and scoop out the flesh. Coarsely chop and transfer the flesh to a mesh sieve; press out extra water with a spoon.
3 Combine the drained eggplant, dressing, tomato, bell pepper, onion, and parsley in a medium bowl. Season with salt and pepper.
4 Transfer the eggplant mixture to a large, shallow serving dish, then top with the reserved parsley leaves; serve.

Tabbouleh

PARSLEY SALAD WITH BULGUR WHEAT

There are a whole lot of flavors going on in this salad, but really, it's all about the parsley…and the parsley in this salad is all about the technique. In order to keep it fresh and crisp, the parsley is washed, completely dried, and then cut into very thin confetti-like strips, called a chiffonade (see Chiffonading Herbs, page 10). The best tool for this job is a very sharp paring knife.

Serves *6*
Preparation Time: *45 minutes*
Cooking Time: *0 minutes*

3 bunches (1 lb/500 g) fresh parsley
½ cup (100 g) fine-ground bulgur wheat
1 cup (250 ml) hot water
Juice of 2-3 lemons (about ½ cup/125 ml)
¾ cup (185 ml) olive oil
1 teaspoon salt
¼ teaspoon freshly ground black pepper
4 sprigs fresh mint leaves, minced
1 onion, minced
3 tomatoes, diced
Romaine lettuce leaves, for serving

1 Wash the parsley and completely dry it. Holding them by the stems, gather a handful of parsley leaves together in one hand. Roll the leaves tightly together and use a sharp paring knife to cut them into thin strips. Repeat this process until all the parsley is chopped.
2 Put the bulgur in a medium bowl and pour the water on top; soak until softened, about 10 minutes. Drain the bulgur in a fine mesh sieve, pressing with the back of a spoon to extract the excess water. Fluff the bulgur with a fork.
3 Whisk together the lemon juice, olive oil, salt, and pepper in a small bowl. Gently combine the parsley, bulgur, mint, onion, tomato, and dressing in a large bowl.
4 Transfer to a serving bowl and serve with lettuce leaves to scoop up the salad.

Middle Eastern Salad

SALATA

This is the everyday salad that's present at most meals; anywhere in the Middle East, if you ask for a salad without specifying what kind, this is what you're likely to get.

Serves *4 to 6*
Preparation Time: *15 minutes*

½ batch LemonyMint Salad Dressing (page 28)
1 cucumber (or 3 to 4 Persian or Japanese cucumbers), diced
1 onion, minced
1 lb (500 g) tomatoes, diced (about 4 medium tomatoes)
1 bunch fresh parsley, minced
4 sprigs fresh mint, minced
¼ teaspoon salt

1 Prepare Lemony Mint Salad Dressing.
2 Stir together all ingredients; serve.

VARIATION
Chopped Salad with Sesame Dressing
SALATIT TAHINA

⅓ cup (80 g) tahini
1 tablespoons fresh lemon juice (or ⅛ teaspoon powdered citric acid/lemon salt)
⅓ cup (80 ml) water
1 English cucumber (or 3 to 4 Persian or Japanese cucumbers), diced
1 onion, minced
1 lb (500 g) tomatoes, diced (about 4 medium tomatoes)
1 bunch fresh parsley, minced
4 sprigs fresh mint, minced
½ teaspoon salt
4 tablespoons olive oil

1 Whisk together the tahini and lemon juice in a medium bowl.
2 Whisk in the water drop-by-drop at first, and then in a thin drizzle (the sauce will thicken at first and then thin into a nice pourable consistency).
3 Stir the tahini dressing together with all remaining ingredients (except the olive oil) in a medium bowl; refrigerate until serving (it's best to let it chill for at least 30 minutes so the flavors can blend).
4 Right before serving, drizzle the olive oil on top.

Spiced Cheese Salad

SALATIT SHANKLEESH

In this salad, the richness of the cheese pairs beautifully with the flavor of fresh vegetables. This dish is wonderful when scooped up with flatbread or spread on crackers. It's a common breakfast dish, but is also an elegant addition to any maza platter.

Serves *4*
Preparation Time: *5 minutes*

1 portion Spiced Cheese Ball (page 69)
1 tomato, diced
2 green onions (scallions), white and green parts thinly sliced
3-4 tablespoons olive oil
1 tablespoon chopped fresh parsley
Flatbread (for serving)

1 Prepare Spiced Cheese Ball.
2 Crumble the cheese into the bottom of a shallow serving dish.
3 Scatter the tomato and onion on top, then drizzle with the olive oil and sprinkle on the parsley.
4 Serve immediately with flatbread.

Herb Salad with Tangy Dressing and Croutons

FATTOUSH

Fattoush is my all-time favorite salad. It's full of fresh herbs like parsley and mint, which thrill the taste buds and give this salad a bright, refreshing flavor. In addition to fresh herbs, another traditional component of Fattoush is purslane (also see called mâché, lamb's tongue, or lamb's lettuce), which is a unique leafy green with a slightly nutty flavor and a hint of bitterness. My mother-in-law likes to dress this salad in the traditional Syrian style with a simple combination of garlic, salt, lemon juice, and olive oil—without sumac and/or pomegranate molasses, which are common additions these days. The last component that really makes this salad Fattoush is croutons, which is the perfect use for stale bread.

The croutons for this salad are made of flatbread and can be prepared in three different ways: oil-fried, toasted, or oven-dried.

Serves *4 to 6*
Preparation Time: *15 minutes*
Cooking Time: *20 minutes (to make the croutons)*

1 batch Lemony Mint Salad Dressing (page 28)
1 large (or 2 small) Arabic flatbread, made into croutons
  (see the headnote)
1 bunch purslane (see purslane on page 22)
½ bunch fresh parsley
¼ bunch fresh mint
1 head Romaine lettuce, shredded
4 green onions (scallions), white and green parts
  thinly sliced
2 Persian or Japanese cucumbers (or ½ of a regular cucumber),
  diced
2 tomatoes, diced and briefly drained in a colander
  if very watery

1 Prepare the Lemony Mint Salad Dressing.
2 Pull the leaves off the herbs and discard the stems. If the leaves are bite-sized, leave them as is; if they are larger than bite-sized, tear them into smaller pieces.
3 To make the croutons, fry the bread in oil, pour a generous coating of olive oil in a large skillet over medium-high heat. Once the oil is hot, add the bread and fry briefly until light golden brown on both sides, flipping once. Transfer the fried bread to a paper towel-lined plate to drain excess oil. Cool bread completely, and then break into bite-sized pieces.
4 To toast the bread, preheat the oven to 375°F (190°C). Cut the bread into bite-sized pieces and toss with a little olive oil. Spread out in a single layer on a large baking sheet and bake until golden brown, about 10 to 15 minutes, stirring the bread once halfway through.
5 To dry the bread in the oven, preheat the oven to 250°F (120°C). Put the whole bread directly onto the oven rack and bake until brittle but not burned, about 15 minutes, flipping once. Cool the bread completely, and then break into bite-sized pieces.
6 Gently toss all the salad ingredients with the dressing and croutons in a large bowl. Serve immediately.

Spicy Potatoes (page 57)

CHAPTER THREE

Vegetable and Rice Side Dishes

Lunch in the Middle East, which is the largest and most formal meal of the day, usually only has one main dish but several side dishes of vegetables (and the more guests that are present, the more sides there are available), so even though they may not be the focus of the meal, they still play a vital role. Many rice dishes—like Upside-Down Rice Casserole (Maqluba) (page 114), Fish Pilaf with Caramelized Onion (Sayadieh bil Samek) (page 86), and Rice Pilaf with Spiced Smoked Chicken (Mendy Dajaj) (page 94)—are main meals in and of themselves and are found in later chapters. The rice dishes in this chapter are typically served with some kind of saucy dish; for example, Saffron Rice with Golden Raisins and Pine Nuts (Roz Mlow'wan) (page 61) is often served with Shrimp in Aromatic Tomato Sauce (Makboos Rubian) (page 95) and Rice with Toasted Vermicelli Noodles (Roz bil Shariya) (page 58) is frequently served with dishes such as Roasted Chicken with Rice and Vegetable Soup (Molokhia Na meh) (page 90), Cauliflower Meat Sauce (M'nezalit Zahara) (page 110), or Lamb and Yogurt Soup (Shakreeyeh) (page 109). A number of factors go into making the perfect pot of rice; for helpful tips, check out Making the Perfect Pot of Rice on page 13.

Fried Eggplant with Garlic and Parsley Dressing

BATINJAN MEKLEH

Fried eggplant is a perfect example of classic Middle Eastern fare: a humble ingredient is simply cooked and paired with a quick sauce to accentuate its flavor.

The first time I had this dish was in a rural area of Syria, called Zabadani. My husband and I were staying with his family in the country for a few days and another family had come to visit. Of course, as is customary, a feast was in order. My mother-in-law made about 15 different dishes that day, and out of all of them this was my favorite. It was at that moment that my mother-in-law realized that my husband and I truly were perfect for each other. You see, my hubby hates eggplant in any form and my mother-in-law has always hoped he'd marry someone who loves it!

If the eggplant is prepped properly, it really doesn't absorb that much oil when fried, but if you prefer, the eggplant can be grilled or broiled instead. For helpful tips, see Cooking Eggplant, (page 11) and Frying Basics, (page 12).

Serves *4 to 6*
Preparation Time: *10 minutes, plus 30 minutes for the eggplant to drain*
Cooking Time: *20 minutes*

1 large or 2 small globe eggplants (about 2 lb/900 g)
2 teaspoons salt
4 tablespoons red wine vinegar
1 tablespoon water
4 cloves garlic, minced
¼ bunch fresh parsley, minced
Oil, for shallow frying

1 Fully or partially peel the eggplant if desired. (To partially peel it, peel one strip off down the length of the vegetable, then leave the next strip in place and peel the next strip off, and so on). Slice into ¼ to ½ inch (6 mm to 1.25 cm) thick slices (lengthwise or crosswise is fine if you're using baby eggplant, but if you're using a large eggplant slice it crosswise).
2 Sprinkle the salt on both sides of each slice and transfer to a colander; put the colander in the sink and let it sit for 30 minutes. Rinse the eggplant under cold running water, then gently wring out any excess water and pat dry.
3 Combine the vinegar, water, garlic, and parsley in a small bowl and set aside.

4 Coat the bottom of a large skillet over moderately high heat with oil. Fry the eggplant in batches (so the pan isn't overcrowded) until golden brown, about 2 to 4 minutes per side. (You can add more oil to the pan if necessary.) Transfer the cooked eggplant to a paper towel-lined plate to drain any excess oil.
5 Serve the eggplant warm or at room temperature, along with the dressing to drizzle on top.

Fresh Tomato Sauce

MUTABBAL YEMENI

This sauce is similar to a cold tomato soup, almost like a Spanish Gazpacho. It's spicy, sweet, and refreshing, and is typically spooned on top of rice dishes such as Rice Pilaf with Spiced Smoked Chicken (page 94).

Yields *about 2 cups (500 ml)*
Preparation Time: *5 minutes*

1 lb (500 g) tomatoes (about 4 medium), sliced
1 small hot green chili pepper, deseeded and sliced
2 cloves garlic, peeled
4 sprigs fresh mint, washed
4 tablespoons water
¼ teaspoon salt

1 Combine all ingredients in a blender or food processor and puree until smooth.
2 Keep refrigerated until ready to serve.

Potatoes with Herbs and Garlic

M'FARAKAT BATATA

Instead of frying the potatoes, you can boil them for this recipe if you prefer. To do so, put the peeled and cubed potato in a medium saucepan and add enough cold water to cover by about 1 inch (2.5 cm). Bring to a boil over high heat, then turn the heat down to medium-low and simmer until fork-tender, about 5 to 7 minutes; drain the potato and toss with the sautéed garlic/cilantro mixture. Or the potatoes can be roasted; preheat oven to 425°F (220°C); toss the peeled and cubed potatoes with 2 tablespoons canola oil in a large bowl; spread in an even layer on a large baking sheet and roast until soft and golden brown, about 20 to 30 minutes, stirring once.

Serves *4*
Preparation Time: *10 minutes*
Cooking Time: *22 minutes*

Oil, for frying
2 lb (1 kg) potatoes, peeled and cubed
4 tablespoons olive oil
4 cloves garlic, crushed in a mortar and pestle with 1 teaspoon salt
½ bunch fresh coriander leaves (cilantro), minced

1 Coat the bottom of a medium saucepan with about ½ inch (1.25 cm) of oil. Heat over medium heat; add half the potato and cook until tender inside and golden outside, about 8 to 10 minutes, stirring occasionally. Transfer the potato to a paper towel-lined plate to drain, and cook the remaining potato the same way.
2 Heat the olive oil in a large nonstick skillet over medium-low heat. Cook the garlic and fresh coriander leaves until the garlic is light golden and the cilantro is wilted, about 3 minutes, stirring frequently.
3 Add the potatoes and cook until warm, about 2 minutes; serve warm or at room temperature.

VARIATION
Herbed Potato Salad

SALATIT BATATA

1 batch Lemony Mint Salad Dressing (page 28)
2 tablespoons fresh lemon juice
¾ teaspoon salt
2 lb (1 kg) potatoes, peeled and cubed
Cold water, to cook the potato
½ bunch fresh parsley, washed and minced
4 sprigs fresh mint, washed and minced
3 green onions (scallions), white and green parts thinly sliced

1 Prepare the Lemony Mint Salad Dressing and whisk with the lemon juice, and salt in a small bowl and set aside.
2 Put the peeled and cubed potato in a medium saucepan and add enough cold water to cover by about 1 inch (2.5 cm). Bring to a boil over high heat, then turn heat down to medium-low and simmer until fork-tender, about 5 to 7 minutes; drain.
3 Add the potato to a large bowl and gently toss with the dressing, parsley, mint, and green onion; serve warm or at room temperature.

Okra with Tomatoes in a Fragrant Sauce

BAMIEH BIL ZAYT

You can use fresh or frozen okra in this dish, depending on whether it's in season or not. If you're using frozen okra, don't thaw it before adding, just add it frozen and simmer for about 10 minutes. If you're using fresh, look for small okra pods since they're tenderer and not as fuzzy. Make sure to clean the okra (you can rub the "fuzz" off with a damp cloth) and trim the stem ends, then simmer for about 10 minutes.

To prevent the okra from becoming slimy, try not to pierce the pods or cut it into pieces; be careful to stir gently so your pods remain intact and be sure not to overcook the okra. Also, the tomatoes in this dish (like anything acidic) help to prevent the okra from becoming slimy.

To make this dish a full meal, cook some type of stew meat (lamb or beef) and add it to the okra before serving.

Serves *4 to 6*
Preparation Time: *12 minutes*
Cooking Time: *35 minutes*

4 tablespoons olive oil
1 large onion, diced
4 cloves garlic, crushed in a mortar and pestle with
 ¾ teaspoon salt
½ teaspoon ground coriander
2 pinches ground cinnamon
1 pinch ground allspice
1 pinch ground nutmeg
1 pinch ground cloves
⅛ teaspoon freshly ground black pepper
3 medium tomatoes, diced
2 tablespoons tomato paste
½ cup (125 ml) water
1 lb (500 g) baby okra (fresh or frozen; if frozen, there's no need to thaw), stem ends trimmed

1 Heat the oil in a large lidded skillet over medium heat; add the onion and cook until softened, about 5 to 7 minutes, stirring occasionally. Add the garlic, coriander, Syrian Spice Mix, and black pepper, and cook 1 minute, stirring constantly.
2 Add the tomatoes, tomato paste, and water and bring up to a boil. Cover the skillet, turn the heat down to simmer, and cook until thickened, about 10 minutes, stirring occasionally.
3 Add the okra, turn the heat up to high, and bring it up to a simmer. Once simmering, cover the skillet, turn the heat down, and simmer until tender, about 10 minutes.
4 Uncover the skillet, turn the heat up to moderately high, and cook until the sauce is thickened, about 2 minutes, stirring frequently.

Fried Cauliflower with Sesame Parsley Sauce

QARNABEET MEKLEH BIL TARATOOR

This is one recipe that will completely surprise you. Normally cauliflower isn't the kind of food I want to plan a whole meal around, but after tasting this dish I find myself craving it and thinking of different meals that would feature it.

After frying, cauliflower takes on a rich, slightly nutty, caramelized flavor; the sesame sauce on top adds the perfect tangy contrast. Scoop the cauliflower up with Arabic flatbread and you have a light meal, but my mother-in-law usually serves this with Aromatic Whole Roasted Fish (Samek Meshwi) (page 87), since the flavor of the sesame sauce complements both dishes.

If you don't want to fry the cauliflower, you can roast it using the method that is described for Cauliflower Meat Sauce (M'nezalit Zahara) (page 110).

Serves *4 to 6*
Preparation Time: *10 minutes*
Cooking Time: *25 minutes*

1 large head cauliflower, cut into florets
Oil, for deep-frying
1 batch Sesame-Parsley Dip (page 25) or Sesame
  Sauce (page 25)

1 Prepare Sesame Sauce or Sesame Parsley Dip.
2 Blanch the cauliflower for 5 minutes in salted boiling water, drain, and pat dry.
3 Fill a large, heavy-bottomed pot ⅓ of the way full with oil; heat the oil to between 350 to 375°F (175 to 190°C) over moderately-high heat.
4 Add ½ of the cauliflower and fry until golden brown, about 6 to 10 minutes, stirring occasionally. Transfer the fried cauliflower to a paper towel-lined plate to drain any excess oil. Repeat this process with the remaining cauliflower.
5 Serve the cauliflower warm or at room temperature, with the Sesame Sauce drizzled on top.

Spicy Potatoes   BATATA HARRA

Sweet bell peppers and ground sweet paprika help to soften the heat factor of this dish, but if you like it extra hot you can add another chili pepper or more ground red pepper (cayenne).

Serves *4*
Preparation Time: *10 minutes*
Cooking Time: *25 minutes*

Oil, for frying
2 lb (1 kg) potatoes, peeled and cubed
4 tablespoons olive oil
1 small onion, diced
1 red bell pepper, deseeded and diced
1 small hot green chili pepper, minced
2 cloves garlic, crushed
1 teaspoon salt
1 teaspoon ground sweet paprika
½ teaspoon ground red pepper (cayenne)
¼ teaspoon freshly ground black pepper
½ bunch fresh coriander leaves (cilantro), minced
2 limes, wedged (for serving)

1 Coat the bottom of a medium saucepan with about ½ inch (1.25 cm) of canola oil. Heat over medium heat; add half the potato and cook until tender inside and golden outside, about 8 to 10 minutes, stirring occasionally. Transfer the potato to a paper towel-lined plate to drain, and cook the remaining potato the same way.
2 Heat the olive oil in a large skillet over medium heat; add the onion, bell pepper, and chili pepper, and cook until they start to soften, about 5 minutes, stirring occasionally.
3 Add the garlic, salt, ground sweet paprika, ground red pepper, and black pepper, and cook until fragrant, about 1 minute, stirring constantly.
4 Add the potatoes and fresh coriander leaves and cook until warm, about 2 minutes. Serve with lime wedges to squeeze on top.

Sautéed Greens With Cilantro

KHOUBEZEH

Dandelion greens are a highly nutritious, bitter green; like purslane (page 22), they are often thought of as a weed, but they are prized in Middle Eastern cuisine. A bowl of sautéed greens is a nice addition to a maza platter; my father-in-law often jokes that he'd rather have a vegetarian meal like this than a whole lamb.

Serves *2 to 3*
Preparation Time: *10 minutes*
Cooking Time: *20 minutes*

1 teaspoon plus a slightly scant ½ teaspoon salt, divided
1 lb (500 g) dandelion greens or mustard greens, tough stems trimmed, washed, and chopped
3 tablespoons olive oil
1 onion, diced
2 cloves garlic, crushed in a mortar and pestle
⅛ teaspoon freshly ground black pepper
1 bunch fresh coriander leaves (cilantro), minced

1 Fill a medium pot ¾ full of water and bring to a boil, then add 1 teaspoon of salt. Add the dandelion greens and blanch them until the stems are tender, about 10 minutes. Drain the greens in a colander, pressing gently with the back of a spoon to extract as much water as possible.
2 Heat the oil in a large skillet over moderately-high heat; add the onion and cook until softened and just starting to brown, about 3 to 4 minutes, stirring occasionally.
3 Stir in the garlic, then add the greens, black pepper, and remaining slightly scant ½ teaspoon salt; cook 2 minutes, then stir in the coriander leaves and cook 1 minute more; serve.

Rice with Toasted Vermicelli Noodles ROZ BIL SHARIYA

When flatbread doesn't accompany a Middle Eastern meal, it's usually because this dish has taken its place. This rice is served alongside many soup, stew, and sauce-based dishes, which are spooned on top of the rice. For tips on cooking rice, see Making the Perfect Pot of Rice (page 13).

Serves *4 to 6*
Preparation Time: *15 minutes*
Cooking Time: *15 minutes, plus 15 minutes to let the rice sit after cooking*

1½ cups (325 g) uncooked medium grain white rice, rinsed
2 tablespoons clarified butter (or 1 tablespoon butter plus 1 tablespoon canola oil)
4 tablespoons dried vermicelli noodles
1¾ cups (425 ml) boiling water
¾ teaspoon salt

1 Soak the rice in tepid water for 10 minutes; drain.
2 While the rice is soaking, put half a kettle of water on to boil.
3 Add the clarified butter to a medium, thick-bottomed lidded saucepan over medium heat. Add the vermicelli and cook until fragrant and light golden brown, about 1 to 2 minutes, stirring constantly.
4 Add the rice to the saucepan with the toasted vermicelli and cook 2 minutes, stirring frequently. Add the boiling water and salt; turn the heat up to high, bring to a rolling boil, and boil 1 minute.
5 Give the rice a stir, then cover the saucepan, turn the heat down to very low, and cook until tender, about 10 to 12 minutes (do not open the lid during this time). Turn the heat off and let the rice sit 15 minutes, then fluff with a fork.

Spiced Green Beans with Tomatoes LOUBIEH BIL ZAYT

I've been eating green beans all my life. I've always liked them well enough, but they never wowed me until I had this dish. The beans take on a slightly nutty flavor from being toasted in olive oil. When paired with the sweetness of the tomato, savory flavor of garlic, and subtle spice notes of cinnamon, allspice, nutmeg, and cloves it leaves me with green bean cravings for the first time in my life.

Serves *4 to 6*
Preparation Time: *15 minutes*
Cooking Time: *45 minutes*

4 tablespoons olive oil
1 large onion, diced
1 lb (500 g) fresh or frozen green beans, stem ends
    trimmed and cut into 1-2 in (2.5-5 cm) pieces
4 cloves garlic, crushed
¾ teaspoon salt
⅛ teaspoon each of ground cinnamon, ground nutmeg,
    ground clove and ground allspice
⅛ teaspoon freshly ground black pepper
3 medium tomatoes, diced
2 tablespoons tomato paste
½ cup (125 ml) water

1 Heat the oil in a large lidded skillet over medium heat; add the onion and cook until softened, about 5 to 7 minutes, stirring occasionally. Add the green beans and sauté until they start to take on a little color, about 10 minutes, stirring occasionally. Add the garlic, Syrian Spice Mix, and black pepper, and cook 1 minute, stirring constantly.
2 Add the tomatoes, tomato paste, and water and bring up to a boil. Cover the skillet, turn the heat down to simmer, and cook until tender, about 20 to 30 minutes, stirring occasionally.
3 Once the beans are tender, uncover the skillet, turn the heat up to moderately high, and cook until the sauce is thickened, about 2 minutes, stirring frequently.

Saffron Rice with Golden Raisins and Pine Nuts

ROZ MLOW'WAN

This vibrant rice dish gets its beautiful color from saffron or turmeric. Sultanas (golden raisins) add a little sweetness and toasted pine nuts add a nice crunch.

Serves *4 to 6*
Preparation Time: *10 minutes*
Cooking Time: *20 minutes, plus 15 minutes to let the rice sit after cooking*

1½ cups (325 g) basmati rice, rinsed
2 tablespoons olive oil
3 tablespoons pine nuts
1 onion, finely diced
4 tablespoons sultanas (golden raisins)
1¾ cups (425 ml) boiling water
¾ teaspoon salt
½ teaspoon saffron threads (or ½ teaspoon turmeric)

1 Soak the rice in tepid water for 10 minutes; drain. While the rice is soaking, put half a kettle of water on to boil.
2 Add the oil to a medium, thick-bottomed lidded sauce-pan over medium heat. Add the pine nuts and cook until golden brown, about 1 to 2 minutes, stirring constantly. Transfer the pine nuts to a small bowl and set aside.
3 Add the onion to the saucepan you cooked the pine nuts in, and cook until softened and just starting to brown, about 5 to 7 minutes, stirring occasionally. Add the rice and cook 2 minutes, stirring frequently. Stir in the sultanas, boiling water, salt, and saffron (or turmeric), turn the heat up to high, and bring it to a rolling boil.
4 Give the rice a stir, then cover the saucepan, turn the heat down to very low, and cook until tender, about 10 minutes (do not open the lid during this time). Turn the heat off and let the rice sit (covered) 15 minutes, then fluff with a fork.
5 Transfer to a serving dish and sprinkle the toasted pine nuts on top; serve.

OPTIONAL
Add two pods of cardamom, two whole cloves, and one 2-inch (5 cm) piece of cinnamon stick at the same time that you add the rice.

VARIATION
Mixed White and Yellow Rice

Serves *4 to 6*
Preparation Time: *10 minutes*
Cooking Time: *20 minutes, plus 15 minutes to let the rice sit after cooking*

1½ cups (325 g) uncooked basmati rice, rinsed
2 tablespoons oil
1 onion, finely diced
1 bay leaf
2 whole cloves
2 pods cardamom, cracked open
2 whole peppercorns
¾ teaspoon salt
1¾ cups (425 ml) boiling water
1-2 pinches saffron threads or ½ teaspoon turmeric dissolved in
    1 tablespoon hot water

1 Soak the rice in tepid water for 10 minutes; drain. While the rice is soaking, put half a kettle of water on to boil.
2 Add the oil to a medium, thick-bottomed lidded saucepan, cover and place over moderately high heat. Once hot, add the onion and cook until softened, about 5 minutes, stirring occasionally.
3 Add the rice, bay leaf, cloves, cardamom pods, peppercorns, and salt, and cook until fragrant, about 2 minutes, stirring frequently. Add the boiling water to the rice, turn heat up to high, and bring it to a rolling boil. Give it a stir, cover the pot, turn heat down to very low, and cook 10 minutes (don't open the lid during this time).
4 After the rice is cooked, let the pot sit with the lid on for 15 minutes, then fluff the rice with a fork. Transfer ⅓ of the rice to a separate bowl.
5 Stir the saffron or turmeric-colored water into ⅓ of the rice (the rice will turn yellow). Mix together the yellow rice and white rice; serve.

Garlicky Potato Dip (page 67)

CHAPTER FOUR

Appetizers and Light Meals

These dishes are the tasty morsels that are frequently thought of as maza, which is basically the equivalent of tapas in Spain. (For more information on maza, see Putting Together Maza Platters, page 14.) It's quite common to group a few of these dishes together (along with maybe a salad and one or two vegetable dishes) for a full meal, especially if you're cooking for just yourself or yourself plus one or two others; however, these dishes can also be served as appetizers before a larger meal. A few of the recipes in this section (the dips in particular) are perfect for using up leftovers; Garlicky Potato Dip (Mutabbal Batata) (page 67) is a delicious use for leftover potato, and both Zucchini Dip (Mutabbal Kousa) (page 64) and Zucchini Fritters (Ejet Kousa) (page 65) are wonderful for using up leftover zucchini.

Eggplant Dip

MUTABBAL BATINJAN

Mutabbal Batinjan, a delicious, creamy eggplant dip with tahini and yogurt, is commonly mistaken for another eggplant-based dip called *Baba Ghanouj*. *Baba Ghanouj* doesn't have tahini or yogurt, but instead has a plethora of fresh veggies mixed in, like green bell pepper, tomato, green onion (scallion), and parsley; lemon, garlic, and occasionally walnuts and pomegranate molasses are also added to *Baba Ghanouj*.

Serves *8*
Preparation Time: *20 minutes*
Cooking Time: *40 minutes*

1 medium globe eggplant (1-1¼ lb/500-600 g)
3 cloves garlic, crushed
1 teaspoon salt
½ cup (125 g) tahini
4 tablespoons fresh lemon juice
4 tablespoons plain yogurt
1 tablespoon thinly sliced walnuts (optional)
Salt, to taste
3 tablespoons olive oil
1 tablespoon minced fresh parsley leaves (optional, for garnish)
Flatbread (for serving)

1 Preheat the oven to 400°F (200°C). Pierce the eggplant a few times with a sharp knife, transfer to a sheet pan, and roast until soft, about 40 minutes. (Alternatively, the whole eggplant can be grilled until tender.) When it's cool enough to handle, cut the eggplant in half lengthwise, scoop out the flesh, and chop it.
2 Mash the eggplant, garlic, salt, tahini, lemon juice, and yogurt together in a large mortar and pestle until it reaches your desired consistency, (it can be completely smooth or you can leave a few lumps for texture; alternatively, this can be done in a food processor). Stir in the walnuts, if using, then taste and add more salt as desired.
3 Transfer to a large, shallow serving dish and drizzle olive oil on top; sprinkle on the parsley, if using.
4 Serve with flatbread to scoop up the dip.

VARIATION
Zucchini Dip *MUTABBAL KOUSA*

This variation is the perfect use for the marrow squash or zucchini insides after you've made Stuffed Marrow Squash (page 107).

Serves *4*
Preparation Time: *10 minutes*
Cooking Time: *15 minutes*

Insides from 2 lb (1 kg) marrow squash or zucchini washed and peeled
2 cloves garlic, crushed
1 teaspoon salt
3 tablespoons plain yogurt
2 tablespoons fresh lemon juice
2 tablespoons olive oil
Fresh parsley or mint leaves (optional, for garnish)
Flatbread (for serving)

1 Place the zucchini/marrow squash in a medium, thick-bottomed saucepan over moderately high heat. Cook (uncovered) until it's soft and the liquid is evaporated, about 15 minutes, stirring frequently; cool.
2 Mash the zucchini/marrow squash, garlic, salt, yogurt, and lemon juice together in a large mortar and pestle until it reaches your desired consistency, (it can be completely smooth or you can leave a few lumps for texture; alternatively, this can be done in a food processor).
3 Transfer to a serving dish, drizzle on the olive oil, and top with fresh parsley or mint leaves, if using.
4 Serve with flatbread to scoop up the dip.

Zucchini Fritters

EJET KOUSA

Whenever my husband and I visit the Middle East and stay with his family, any morning we wake up to one of my mother-in-law's egg dishes we know it will be a good day. These fritters are basically savory pancakes; they're scented with garlic and onion and a stack of them is all it takes to bring a smile to my face in the morning. They're great served hot, warm, or room temperature, and I like them with olives, fresh tomatoes, and a stack of flatbread.

Serves *4 as a part of a maza platter or 2 as a meal*
Preparation Time: *10 minutes*
Cooking Time: *20 minutes*

2 tablespoons olive oil
1 onion, diced
¾ lb (350 g) zucchini (about 1 medium), grated
2 large cloves garlic, crushed in a mortar and pestle
  with 1 teaspoon salt
4 large eggs
4 tablespoons all-purpose flour
½ bunch fresh parsley, minced
Pinch of freshly ground black pepper
Canola oil, for frying

1 Heat the olive oil in a medium skillet over medium heat; add the onion and cook until it starts to soften, about 5 minutes, stirring occasionally. Add the zucchini and cook until softened and the water has evaporated, about 8 minutes, stirring occasionally; add the garlic and cook 1 minute more, stirring constantly. Cool slightly.
2 Lightly beat together the eggs, flour, parsley, and black pepper in a medium bowl. Stir in the zucchini mixture.
3 Add enough canola oil to a large nonstick skillet to lightly coat the bottom; heat the oil over medium heat.
4 Drop the batter into the hot pan using a small (about 2 tablespoon) or large (about 4 tablespoon) scoop. Fry until set and golden on one side, about 2 minutes; flip and cook until set and golden on the other side, about 1 minute.
5 Transfer the cooked fritters to a paper towel-lined plate to drain any excess oil, and cook the remaining egg mixture the same way, adding more oil to the skillet as necessary.

Eggs Poached in Spicy Tomato Sauce JUZMUZ

There are different versions of this dish all across the Middle East; this is the Syrian version, taught to me by my mother-in-law, which I think is particularly delicious. The sauce is a great balance of sweet, heat, and spicy flavors. The best way to eat this dish is to break open the egg yolk and then eat with flatbread.

Serves *4 as part of a maza platter or 2 as a meal*
Preparation Time: *15 minutes*
Cooking Time: *25 minutes*

2 tablespoons olive oil
1 green bell pepper, deseeded and diced
1 small onion, diced
1 small hot green chili pepper, minced
2 cloves garlic, crushed
½ teaspoon salt
2 tomatoes, diced
1 teaspoon ground cumin
½ teaspoon ground turmeric
½ teaspoon ground paprika
¼ teaspoon ground red pepper (cayenne)
⅛ teaspoon freshly ground black pepper
1 tablespoon tomato paste
½ cup (125 ml) water
4 large eggs
1 sprig fresh parsley, chopped (optional, for garnish)

1 Heat the oil in a medium lidded skillet over medium heat; add the bell pepper and onion and cook until softened, about 5 to 7 minutes, stirring occasionally.
2 Add the chili pepper, garlic, salt, and tomato, and cook 2 minutes; stir in the cumin, turmeric, ground sweet paprika, ground red pepper, and black pepper. Cook 1 minute more.
3 Add the tomato paste and water and bring up to a boil; cover the skillet, turn the heat down to simmer, and cook 10 minutes, stirring occasionally (during the last minute, remove the lid so the sauce can thicken and stir constantly).
4 Use the back of a spoon to make 4 wells in the sauce, and then crack 1 egg into each well. Cover the skillet and cook until the egg whites are set and the yolks are cooked to your desired doneness (about 5 minutes will produce set whites with runny yolks).
5 Sprinkle on the parsley, if using; serve immediately.

Garlicky Potato Dip

MUTABBAL BATATA

In the Middle East, anything and everything you can think of is turned into dip, from avocado to beans, cheese, and zucchini. Many of these dip recipes were created to use up leftovers, but whether or not you have leftover potato, this dip is definitely worth making.

Serves *8*
Preparation Time: *5 minutes, plus 20 minutes for the potatoes to cool*
Cooking Time: *35 minutes*

2 potatoes (about 1 lb/500 g), washed
2 cloves garlic, crushed
¾ cup (185 ml) plain yogurt
4 tablespoons tahini
1 tablespoon fresh lemon juice
½ teaspoon salt
1 tablespoon olive oil
Pinch ground red pepper (cayenne)
Fresh coriander leaves (cilantro) (optional, for garnish)

1 Put the potatoes in a medium saucepan and add enough water to cover them by 1 inch (2.5 cm). Bring up to a boil over high heat, then turn heat down to medium and cook until a paring knife slides right out when inserted fully into the middle of the potato, about 30 minutes.
2 Cool 20 minutes, then peel the potatoes and transfer the flesh to a medium bowl; coarsely mash with a fork.
3 Add the garlic, salt, yogurt, tahini, lemon juice, and salt to the potatoes; stir with a fork to combine, being careful not to over-mix. Combine the olive oil and ground red pepper in a small bowl.
4 Transfer the dip to a serving bowl and drizzle the olive oil/ground red pepper mixture on top; garnish with fresh coriander leaves, if using.

Herbed Omelets   EJEH

These omelets are loaded with fresh herbs, for a bright, fresh flavor.

Serves *4 as part of a maza platter or 2 as a meal*
Preparation Time: *10 minutes*
Cooking Time: *10 minutes*

4 large eggs
2 tablespoons all-purpose flour
¼ teaspoon salt
⅛ teaspoon freshly ground black pepper
½ bunch fresh parsley, minced
2 green onions (scallions), white and green parts, thinly sliced
2 sprigs fresh mint, stems discarded and leaves chopped
Oil, for frying

1 Lightly beat together the eggs, flour, salt, pepper, parsley, green onions, and mint in a medium bowl.
2 Add enough oil to a small nonstick skillet to lightly coat the bottom; heat the oil over medium heat.
3 Pour ¼ cup (65 ml) of the egg mixture into the hot oil and rotate the pan to spread it out. Fry until set on one side, about 1 to 2 minutes; flip and cook until set on the other side, about 30 seconds to 1 minute.
4 Remove the omelet, and cook the remaining egg mixture the same way, adding more oil to the skillet as necessary (you will end up with 4 omelets).
5 Serve warm.

Pan Seared White Cheese

JIBNEH MEKLEH

The first time I had cheese prepared like this was at a restaurant in Amman. It was part of a maza platter and my husband ordered sweet tea to pair with the salty cheese.

Serves *4*
Preparation Time: *2 minutes, plus 2 to 4 hours to soak the cheese*
Cooking Time: *5 minutes*

Two thick slices (6 oz/175 g) Halloumi, Nabulsi, or Ackawi
   cheese, or fresh mozzarella sliced into ¼-½ in (6 mm-1.25 cm)
   thick slabs
1-2 tablespoons flour
1 tablespoon clarified butter (or ½ tablespoon unsalted butter
   plus ½ tablespoon canola oil)
Flatbread (for serving)
Olives and fresh tomato slices

1 To remove excess salt (if using Halloumi, Nabulsi, or Ackawi) soak the cheese in cold water for 2 to 4 hours (or overnight), changing the water several times; pat dry.
2 Coat the cheese with flour and gently rub off any excess.
3 Melt the clarified butter in a medium skillet over medium heat. Add the cheese and fry until golden brown on both sides, about 1 to 2 minutes per side.
4 Serve immediately, with flat bread and olives and/or tomato slices, if using.

Spiced Cheese Balls

SHANKLEESH

Traditionally, these cheese balls are left to ripen and mold for weeks (being periodically rinsed) before they are coated with spices and served, which takes a considerably longer time than my version.

Yields *10 servings*
Preparation Time: *20 minutes, plus 3 days to drain the yogurt and let the balls refrigerate*
Cooking Time: *5 minutes*

4 lb (2 kg) plain yogurt
¾ teaspoon salt
2 teaspoons dried oregano
1 teaspoon ground sweet paprika
½ teaspoon ground red pepper (cayenne)
¼ teaspoon freshly ground black pepper
1 tablespoon Thyme Spice Mix (page 29) (for coating)
½ tablespoon ground sweet paprika and ½ tablespoon ground red pepper (cayenne) (for coating)

1 Prepare Thyme Spice Mix.
2 Put the yogurt in a medium, heavy-bottomed saucepan over medium heat; cook (without stirring) until the curds and whey separate, about 5 minutes. Cool to room temperature.
3 Place a fine mesh sieve inside a bowl and place 2 pieces of cheesecloth or 3 coffee liners inside the sieve so that they drape over the sides. Pour in the yogurt and wrap the cheesecloth or coffee liners up over the top of the yogurt.
4 Cover the top with plastic wrap, place a heavy bowl or other object on top (to help it drain faster), and let it drain like this in the fridge for 2 days, pouring out the whey that collects in the bowl as necessary.
5 Combine the drained yogurt curds with the salt, oregano, paprika, cayenne, and black pepper in a medium bowl. Shape this mixture into 2 equal balls and transfer to a paper towel-lined tray and refrigerate 1 day, changing the paper towels once.
6 Roll 1 ball in Thyme Spice Mix and the other ball in the paprika/cayenne mixture, then cover and store refrigerated until serving.
7 Serve with olive oil and flatbread, or make them into Spiced Cheese Ball Salad (page 47).

VARIATION
Farmer's Cheese Spiced Cheese Balls

For a fun and tasty version of this recipe that's even faster, I use farmer's cheese instead of yogurt, which eliminates the need to separate the curds from the whey. If you're using Nabulsi or Ackawi cheese, do not add any salt; if you're using fresh mozzarella, add salt to taste (about ½ to ¾ teaspoon).

¼ lb (100 g) Nabulsi, Ackawi, or fresh mozzarella cheese
¾ lb (350 g) farmer's cheese
2 teaspoons dried oregano
1 teaspoon ground sweet paprika
½ teaspoon ground red pepper (cayenne)
¼ teaspoon freshly ground black pepper
1 tablespoon Thyme Spice Mix (page 29) (for coating)
½ tablespoon ground sweet paprika and ½ tablespoon ground red pepper (cayenne) (for coating)

1 If you're using Nabulsi or Ackawi cheese, remove the saltiness by soaking the cheese in cold water for 2 to 4 hours (or overnight), changing the water several times; pat dry.
2 Finely crumble the Nabulsi or Ackawi with your fingers, or grate the mozzarella; combine it with the farmer's cheese, oregano, paprika, cayenne, and black pepper in a medium bowl. Shape this mixture into 2 equal balls and transfer to a paper towel-lined tray and refrigerate 1 day, changing the paper towels once.
3 Roll 1 ball in Thyme Spice Mix and the other ball in the paprika/cayenne mixture, then cover and store refrigerated until serving.
4 Serve with olive oil and flatbread, or make them into Spiced Cheese Ball Salad (page 47).

How to Stuff Grape Leaves

STEP 1: Place 2 to 3 teaspoons of filling across the leaf above the point where the stem was cut off.

STEP 2: Fold bottom of the leaf up over the stuffing.

STEP 3: Fold over the sides of the leaf onto the stuffing.

STEP 4: Roll up the leaf, tucking in the sides as you go.

Vegetarian Stuffed Grape Leaves — WARAQ AL AINAB OR DAWALI

Grape leaves (or vine leaves) can be stuffed with either a vegetable or meat-based rice stuffing. This recipe is the vegetarian version, which is light and fresh, more like a salad than anything else. The version with meat is typically served hot as a main course (for the recipe, see Lamb and Rice Stuffing (Heshweh) on page 28); this vegetarian variation is usually served at room temperature, as part of a maza platter. (*Note*: When the stuffed grape leaves are cooked, a heavy, flat, disk-shaped object must be placed into the pot to weigh the leaves down and keep them submerged beneath the liquid. In Arabic, this tool is called a *Teteelet Fakhar*, but any heat-safe lid or plate that fits nicely into your pot will work.)

Serves *8 to 10*
Preparation Time: *2 hours, plus 3 hours for the rice mixture to soak before stuffing the leaves and time for the stuffed grape leaves to cool before serving*
Cooking Time: *1 hour, 45 minutes*

1½ cups (325 g) uncooked medium-grain white rice, rinsed
3 tablespoons oil
1 onion, finely diced
2½ teaspoons salt, divided
2 tomatoes, finely diced
1 bunch fresh parsley, minced
6 tablespoons (90 ml) fresh lemon juice, divided
4 tablespoons olive oil, divided
4 tablespoons dried, crushed mint
One (1 lb/500 g) jar of brined grape leaves, rinsed (see Grape Leaves, page 20)
2 medium potatoes, peeled and sliced
Hot water, to cook the grape leaves
Plain yogurt (optional, for serving)
2 lemons, wedged (optional, for serving)

1 Soak the rice in tepid water for 10 minutes; drain.
2 Heat the oil in a large skillet over medium heat; add the onion and 1 teaspoon salt, and sauté until the onion starts to soften, about 3 to 5 minutes. Cool completely.
3 Combine the onion, remaining 1¼ teaspoons salt, tomato, parsley, 3 tablespoons lemon juice, 2 tablespoons olive oil, mint, and rice in a large bowl; cover the bowl and refrigerate 3 hours.
4 Soak the grape leaves in hot water for 10 minutes, changing the water twice; drain. Trim off the stems, if necessary.
5 To stuff the grape leaves, lay 1 leaf flat on your work surface with the shiny side facing down. Place 2 to 3 teaspoons of filling (adjust the amount based on the size of your leaves) across the leaf above the point where the stem was cut off. Fold the bottom of the leaf up over the stuffing, and then fold over the sides of the leaf onto the stuffing. Roll up the leaf, tucking in the sides as you go. Continue this way until all the leaves are stuffed. (*Note*: If you have any leaves that are very small, you can place 2 leaves overlapping and stuff them.)
6 Line the bottom of a medium-large, thick-bottomed, lidded pot with the potato. Arrange the grape leaves (seam-side down) in compact rows on top of the potatoes, continuing with additional layers until all the grape leaves are in the pan.
7 Sprinkle the remaining 3 tablespoons of lemon juice, remaining 2 tablespoons of olive oil, and remaining ¼ teaspoon salt on top of the leaves; place a heavy, flat, disc-shaped object (such as a heat-safe lid or plate) into the pan on top of the leaves. Add enough hot water to cover the leaves by 2 inches (5 cm).
8 Bring to a boil over high heat, then cover the pot, turn the heat down to low, and simmer until the rice is tender, about 1 hour, 15 minutes to 1 hour, 45 minutes; cool.
9 To serve, drain the stuffed grape leaves in a large colander, reserving the liquid in a bowl under the colander (store any leftovers in this liquid). Arrange on a platter and serve at room temperature, along with plain yogurt and lemon wedges, if using.

Bell Pepper Walnut Dip

MUHAMMARA

Peppers grow in abundance in Aleppo, Syria, which is where this dish comes from. Walnuts, pomegranate molasses, and sumac are ingredients that make this dish rich and nutty, with a sweet/tart yet also savory and spicy flavor. In many dishes, whether or not the breadcrumbs are fresh really doesn't make a big difference. This is not one of those dishes. Rather, this dip really benefits from taking the extra couple of minutes to make the breadcrumbs. To do so, tear a slightly stale piece of flatbread into large pieces; put it in the food processor and pulse until it forms breadcrumbs. Any extra breadcrumbs you have can be stored in zipper-top plastic bag in the freezer for up to 6 months. (Note: The amount of breadcrumbs can be increased if you prefer a thicker dip.)

Serves *6 to 8*
Preparation Time: *25 minutes*
Cooking Time: *10 minutes*

3 red bell peppers, halved and deseeded
2 tablespoons olive oil
½ cup (50 g) chopped walnuts
2 cloves garlic, peeled
1 small onion, chopped
1 tablespoon pomegranate molasses
¾ teaspoon salt
½ teaspoon ground red pepper (cayenne)
½ teaspoon ground cumin
½ teaspoon ground sumac
¼ teaspoon freshly ground black pepper
¼ cup (20 g) fresh bread crumbs
Fresh parsley or mint leaves (optional, for garnish)

1 Preheat the broiler. Put each pepper half skin-side-up on a flat surface and press down with your hand to flatten. Transfer to a baking sheet and broil until the skin is blackened and blistered (about 10 to 12 minutes). Immediately transfer the peppers to a bowl and cover (or to a large, zipper-top plastic bag) and let them sit 15 minutes. Peel off skin (do not rinse) and coarsely chop peppers; drain off any excess water.
2 Combine the bell pepper, olive oil, walnuts, garlic, onion, pomegranate molasses, salt, cayenne, cumin, sumac, and black pepper in the bowl of a food processor; pulse until it comes together as a chunky paste, scraping down the sides of the bowl as necessary. Pulse in the breadcrumbs. (Alternatively, this can be done by hand using a large mortar and pestle.)
3 Transfer to a serving dish and garnish with fresh parsley or mint leaves, if using.

Yogurt Cheese

LABNEH

Yogurt Cheese is soft and creamy with a mild, tangy flavor. It can frequently be found spread inside sandwiches or as part of a maza platter for breakfast along with olives, fresh mint, flatbread, olive oil, Thyme Spice Mix (page 29), and some sliced tomato, cucumber, and/or green onion. The best way to serve Yogurt Cheese is to spread it into a shallow bowl and top it with a generous douse of olive oil; anything you add to flavor it beyond that (such as dried mint or other spices) is up to you.

Yields *14 oz (400 g) of cheese and 2 cups (500 ml) of whey*
Preparation Time: *5 minutes, plus 1 to 2 days to let the yogurt drain*

2 lb (1 kg) plain yogurt
1 tablespoon olive oil (for serving)
A pinch of dried mint (optional, for serving)

1 Place a fine mesh sieve inside a bowl and place 2 pieces of cheesecloth or 3 coffee liners inside the sieve so that they drape over the sides. Pour in the yogurt and wrap the cheesecloth or coffee liners up over the top of the yogurt.
2 Cover the top with plastic wrap, place a heavy bowl or other object on top (to help it drain faster), and let it drain like this in the fridge for 1 to 2 days, pouring out the whey that collects in the bowl as necessary.
3 To serve, transfer to a shallow bowl, drizzle the olive oil on top, and sprinkle on the mint, if using.

VARIATION
Yogurt Cheese Balls in Oil

LABNEH M'DOWARA

Yields *about 10 to 12 cheese balls*
Preparation Time: *20 minutes, plus 6 days to drain the yogurt and let the balls refrigerate*

2 lb (1 kg) plain yogurt
2 teaspoons salt
Enough olive oil to cover the cheese balls (about 1¼ cups/300 ml total)
4-5 olives to garnish when serving

1 Combine the yogurt and salt in a medium bowl. Line another medium bowl with 2 pieces of cheesecloth; pour the yogurt onto the cheesecloth and tie the ends of the cheesecloth together (or tie it closed with string). Tie the cheesecloth to a long spoon and lay the spoon across the top of a deep bowl or pot (making sure that the cheesecloth doesn't touch the bottom). Let it drain like this for 4 days in the fridge, pouring out the whey that collects in the bottom each day.
2 Roll the strained yogurt into balls about 1½ tablespoons each. Transfer to a paper towel-lined tray and refrigerate 1 day, changing the paper towels once.
3 Sterilize a 1-pint (500 ml) canning jar; transfer the balls to the sterilized jar and add oil (half olive and half canola) to cover; refrigerate 1 day before eating. Store refrigerated.

Falafel (page 81)

CHAPTER FIVE

⊷Beans and Lentils⊷

I haven't had anyone in the Middle East tell me that they're vegetarian, but even so, the Middle Eastern diet typically naturally consists of several vegetarian meals a week. (Of course not when a guest is present though; Meat is usually the most expensive part of a meal and so it is thought that providing a meal containing one, two, or even several meat based dishes shows your generosity to your guests.) However, a meal comprised of a few different vegetable dishes isn't uncommon for a simple family dinner, and neither is a meal of eggs. In addition to vegetables and eggs, beans and lentils are another vegetarian dietary staple, and they're used in a multitude of dishes. Perhaps the most commonly known Middle Eastern bean based dishes are Falafel (page 81) and Hummus (Hummous bil Tahina or M'sebaha) (page 79), and Creamy Chickpea and Yogurt Casserole (Tissiyeh or Fetteh bil Hummous) (page 80) is maybe the Middle East's most delicious best kept secret.

Mashed Fava Beans with Olive Oil, Lemon Juice and Garlic — FOUL MUDAMMAS

This dish comes from Egypt and spread across the Middle East. It's commonly eaten for breakfast, especially on Fridays (which is considered the weekend there), similar to a breakfast of pancakes on Sunday morning in the U.S.

Serves *4*
Preparation Time: *10 minutes*
Cooking Time: *5 minutes*

One (15 oz) can fava beans (sometimes called broad beans), with liquid
One (15 oz/425 g) can chickpeas, rinsed and drained
½ cup (125 ml) water
2 cloves garlic, crushed
½ teaspoon salt
1 tablespoon fresh lemon juice
1 teaspoon ground cumin
¼ teaspoon freshly ground black pepper
4 tablespoons olive oil
1 small tomato, diced
½ small onion, minced
4 tablespoons minced fresh parsley leaves
1 lemon, wedged

1 Bring the fava beans (with liquid), chickpeas, and water to a simmer in a medium saucepan over medium heat. Turn off heat and use the back of a spoon to mash some of the beans (about ½ cup) against the side of the pot.
2 Stir in the garlic, salt, lemon juice, cumin, and black pepper.
3 Transfer the beans to 1 large or 4 small serving dishes; drizzle on the olive oil and arrange the tomato, onion, and parsley on top in a decorative way.
4 Serve with lemon wedges to squeeze on top.

Simple Lentil Soup

SHORABET ADAS

In Middle Eastern cuisine, there typically are no first courses, although that's not to say that soups are not eaten. Most soups are heartier and more stew-like, and are spooned over rice and eaten as a main course. Of course there are exceptions to every rule, and the month-long fast of Ramadan is a time for culinary exceptions. After fasting all day, the fast is broken at sundown with a couple of dates and a sip of water; then comes the first course, which is usually some kind of soup. Red lentil is the soup of choice because it's delicious in its simplicity, and it's hearty and filling enough to prevent you from over-eating during the rest of the meal. Outside of the month of Ramadan, this soup is more frequently eaten as a light meal rather than a first course.

Serves *4 as a first course or 2 as a meal*
Preparation Time: *5 minutes*
Cooking Time: *35 minutes*

1 tablespoon olive oil
1 onion, diced
1 cup (180 g) dried lentils
2 chicken-flavored soft bouillon cubes
2 bay leaves
2 teaspoons cumin
¼ teaspoon freshly ground black pepper
3-4 cups (750 ml-1 liter) hot water
1 lemon, wedged (for serving)
Fresh parsley leaves (optional, for garnish)

1 Heat the oil in a medium saucepan over medium heat; once hot, add the onion and sauté until softened, about 5 to 7 minutes, stirring occasionally.
2 Add the lentils, bouillon cubes, bay leaves, cumin, black pepper and 3 cups (750 ml) hot water. Cover the saucepan, turn heat up to high, and bring the soup up to a rolling boil.
3 Turn heat down to low and simmer 20 to 30 minutes, stirring occasionally and adding up to 1 cup (250 ml) more water as necessary if the soup becomes too thick.
4 Garnish with parsley, if using, and serve with fresh lemon wedges to squeeze on top.

Hummus with Several Variations

HUMMOUS BIL TAHINA OR M'SEBAHA

There are only two bean-based dishes for which I avoid using canned beans, and this recipe is one of them (the other is Falafel on page 81). Even though cooking dried beans takes much longer, the flavor and texture is well worth it in the end for this dish. But I will say that if you are really pressed for time, canned chickpeas will still work. If you're using canned, use 2½ cups; be sure to rinse and drain the chickpeas before using, and reduce the amount of salt.

Yields *about 3 cups (675 g)*
Preparation Time: *10 minutes, plus 12 to 24 hours to soak the chickpeas*
Cooking Time: *2 hours*

1 cup (½ lb/250 g) dried chickpeas
⅓ cup (80 g) tahini
4 tablespoons fresh lemon juice
1 teaspoon ground cumin
2 large cloves garlic, crushed
¾ teaspoon salt
4-8 tablespoons water, or more as needed
4 tablespoons olive oil
Pinch ground sumac (optional, for garnish)
Flatbread (for serving)

1 Soak the chickpeas in cold water for 12 to 24 hours; drain. After soaking, add the chickpeas to a medium pot with fresh water; bring to a boil, then turn the heat down slightly and cook until they're easy to mash with your fingers, about 1 to 2 hours; adding more water as necessary so that they're always immersed; drain. Pick through the beans to remove any skins you find. Measure out 3 to 4 tablespoons of chickpeas and set aside for topping, if desired.
2 Pulse the chickpeas a few times in a food processor until they are lumpy. Add the tahini, lemon juice, cumin, and garlic, salt, and pulse a few times. Add the water one tablespoon at a time with the food processor on, and continue processing until you achieve your desired consistency.
3 Transfer to a shallow serving bowl and drizzle the olive oil on top. Sprinkle the sumac and reserved chickpeas on top, if using. Serve with flatbread for dipping.

VARIATION 1
Hummus with Pine Nuts

1 batch Hummus
4 tablespoons pine nuts

Prepare the Hummus but instead of drizzling the oil on top of the hummus, add it to a small skillet over medium heat. Add the pine nuts and cook until golden brown, about 1 to 2 minutes, stirring constantly. Cool slightly, then pour on top of the hummus; sprinkle the sumac on top, if using.

VARIATION 2
Hummus with Ground Meat

1 batch Hummus (reduce olive oil to 2 tablespoons; omit sumac)
1 small onion, finely diced
¼ lb (100 g) lean ground lamb or beef
¼ teaspoon salt
Pinch each of ground cinnamon, ground allspice, ground clove, and ground nutmeg
Pinch freshly ground black pepper
2 tablespoons pine nuts

Prepare the Hummus according to the recipe. Heat the 2 tablespoons of olive oil in a medium skillet over medium heat; add the onion and sauté until starting to soften, about 3 to 5 minutes, stirring occasionally. Add the ground meat, salt, Syrian Spice Mix, and black pepper; turn heat up to high and cook until the meat is fully browned and the onion is tender, about 3 to 5 minutes, stirring occasionally. Stir in the pine nuts and cook 2 minutes more, stirring occasionally. Cool slightly, then pour on top of the hummus.

Creamy Chickpea and Yogurt Casserole

TISSIYEH

This dish is truly a Damascene delight. People in and around Damascus send their children with a bowl (traditionally a deep glass dish) to a hummus shop and the shopkeeper fills it with bread, chickpeas, and yogurt. Payment is based on the bowl's size, and child returns home with a hot meal for the family.

Serves *4 to 6*
Preparation Time: *5 minutes*
Cooking Time: *25 minutes*

3 large (or 6 small) flatbreads
Two (16 oz/450 g) cans chickpeas
2 cups (500 ml) water
2 teaspoons ground cumin, divided
3½ cups (850 g) plain yogurt
½ cup (125 g) tahini
4 tablespoons fresh lemon juice
4 cloves garlic, crushed
1 teaspoon salt
4 tablespoons olive oil or clarified butter
4 tablespoons pine nuts
1 tablespoon minced fresh parsley leaves
   (optional, for garnish)

1 Preheat oven to 250°F (120°C). Put the whole bread directly onto the oven rack and bake until brittle but not burned, about 15 minutes, flipping once. Cool the bread completely, and then break into bite-sized pieces. Line the bottom of 1 large serving bowl (or 4 individual bowls) with the bread and set aside.
2 Pour the chickpeas (along with their liquid), water, and 1 teaspoon of cumin into a medium saucepan; bring to a simmer over medium heat. Ladle a bit (about 1 to 1½ cups/250 to 375 ml) of the chickpea cooking liquid onto the dried bread to make it moist, but not soggy, pressing down with a spoon to help the bread absorb the liquid. If you add too much liquid, just drain off any excess. Remove 4 tablespoons of chickpeas to a small bowl and set aside, and spoon the remainder of the chickpeas onto the moistened bread.
3 Whisk together the yogurt, tahini, lemon juice, garlic, salt, ½ cup chickpea cooking liquid, and the remaining 1 teaspoon of cumin in a medium bowl. Pour the yogurt mixture onto the chickpeas and sprinkle the remaining 4 tablespoons of chickpeas on top.
4 Heat the oil in a small skillet over medium heat; add the pine nuts and cook until golden brown, about 1 to 2 minutes, stirring constantly; set aside. Drizzle the pine nuts and their oil on top, and sprinkle on the parsley, if using. Serve immediately.

Falafel

There's so much to love about Falafel, even beyond its delicious flavor. Its crunchy exterior and soft, pillow-y interior is a fantastic combination, plus, it's a wonderful vegetarian meal that's full of fiber and protein. It can be eaten as part of a maza platter with hummus, olives, salad, and flatbread, or made into a sandwich. In Damascus, my favorite falafel shop makes a to-die-for falafel sandwich; they use very thin bread (almost as thin as crepes) and add tahini, pomegranate molasses, pickled vegetables, fresh vegetables, and fresh herbs (mint is the main one!). It might not sound like anything special but it keeps me coming back for more when I'm in Damascus…and craving Falafel when I'm across the world.

I like my Falafel a bit heavy on the garlic, so I use three (or four) large cloves; adjust this to suit your tastes. Also, regarding the fresh parsley leaves in the batter, you can substitute fresh cilantro leaves (or use half and half) if you prefer. In the recipe below I instruct you to stir in the parsley after pulsing the batter in a food processor; however, if you want your Falafel to be light green inside, pulse the minced herb into the batter a couple times while it's still in the food processor, and then proceed with the recipe as written.

As for shaping the Falafel, there are special falafel molds you can buy, but I prefer a simpler method: scoop up a bit of batter with one spoon, then pick up another spoon with your other hand; gently scrape the spoons against each other to form oblong-shaped Falafels.

Serves *4 to 6*
Preparation Time: *1 hour, 15 minutes,*
  plus 12 to 24 hours to soak the chickpeas
Cooking Time: *2 hours, 30 minutes*

1 cup (½ lb/250 g) dried chickpeas
1 onion, finely diced
3-4 large cloves garlic, crushed
1 teaspoon salt
1 teaspoon cumin
½ teaspoon dried red pepper flakes
¼ bunch fresh parsley leaves, minced
½ teaspoon baking powder
4-6 tablespoons all-purpose flour
Oil, for frying
Sesame Sauce (page 25) (optional, for serving)
1 tablespoon minced fresh parsley leaves
  (optional, for serving)

1 Prepare the Sesame Sauce.
2 Soak the chickpeas in cold water for 12 to 24 hours; drain. After soaking, add them to a medium pot with fresh water; bring up to a boil, then turn the heat down slightly and cook until they're easy to mash with your fingers, about 1 to 2 hours; adding more water as necessary so that they're always immersed; drain. Pick through the beans to remove any skins you find.
3 Add the chickpeas, onion, garlic, salt, cumin, and red pepper flakes to a food processor and pulse until it forms a chunky paste (do not purée it; alternatively, this can be done by hand using a large mortar and pestle). Transfer to a large bowl and stir in the parsley. Sprinkle in the baking powder and gradually add enough flour to form a dough, being careful not to over-mix. Cover the bowl and refrigerate 1 hour.
4 Add about 3 inches (7.5 cm) of oil to a medium saucepan; heat the oil to between 350 to 375°F (175 to 190°C). As the oil heats, shape the fritters with a Falafel mold or with 2 spoons, gently scraping them against each other to form oblong shaped falafels.
5 Fry the Falafel in batches so the pan doesn't get overcrowded. Fry each batch until golden brown outside and fully cooked inside, about 4 to 6 minutes, and then transfer to a paper towel-lined plate to drain any excess oil. Repeat this process until all the batter is fried.
6 Serve immediately, with a drizzle of Sesame Sauce and a sprinkle of parsley on top, if using.

Lentil and Bulgur Pilaf with Caramelized Onion

MUJADDARA BURGHUL

This hearty pilaf is commonly eaten as a vegetarian meal, with little else besides a bowl of plain yogurt and maybe some sliced tomato, cucumber, and/or onion to accompany it. It's eaten in many Middle Eastern countries and my husband remembers children singing a song about it in middle school while growing up in Syria.

For an easy variation on this dish, use white or brown rice instead of bulgur wheat.

Serves *4 to 6*
Preparation Time: *10 minutes*
Cooking Time: *50 minutes, plus 10 minutes to let the bulgur sit after cooking*

1⅓ cups (275 g) dried brown lentils
   (or 2 cans brown lentils, rinsed and drained)
6 cups (1.5 liters) water
2 tablespoons olive oil
2 tablespoons butter
2 large onions, quartered and thinly sliced
1 bay leaf
2 pods cardamom, cracked open
2 cloves
2 teaspoons ground cumin
½ teaspoon ground cinnamon
1½ teaspoons salt
¼ teaspoon freshly ground black pepper
1 cup (185 g) coarse-ground bulgur wheat
1½ cups (300 ml) boiling water
Plain yogurt (optional, for serving)

1 Sort through the lentils to remove any small stones or pieces of dirt, and then rinse with cold water in a colander. Bring the rinsed lentils and the water to a boil in a lidded medium saucepan. Cover the saucepan, turn the heat down to a simmer, and cook until the lentils are tender but not mushy, about 20 to 30 minutes, stirring occasionally and adding more water as necessary so that they're always immersed; strain.

2 While the lentils cook, heat the oil and the butter in a large skillet over moderately-high heat; add the onion and sauté until completely softened but not yet browned, about 10 minutes, stirring occasionally. Transfer half the onion to a small bowl and set aside. Continue cooking the remaining onion until deep caramel in color, about 5 to 10 minutes, stirring occasionally and adding a splash of water as necessary if the onion starts to get too dark. Set aside.

3 Put half a kettle of water on to boil. Transfer the sautéed onion (not the caramelized onion) to a medium saucepan. Add the bay leaf, cardamom, clove, cumin, cinnamon, salt, and pepper and cook 1 minute. Add the bulgur and cook 1 minute more, stirring constantly. Add the boiling water, turn the heat up to high, and bring to a rolling boil.

4 Give the bulgur a stir, then cover the saucepan, turn the heat down to very low, and cook until tender, about 10 minutes (do not open the lid during this time). Turn the heat off and let the bulgur sit 10 minutes, then fluff with a fork and gently stir in the lentils. Taste and add additional salt, pepper, and olive oil if desired.

5 Transfer to a serving dish and top with the caramelized onion. Serve with plain yogurt to spoon on top, if using.

Lentil Stew with Swiss Chard and Lemon Juice

ADAS BIL HAMUD

Although there are a few minor differences, I like to think of this as the soup version of Sautéed Greens and Cilantro (page 58). This sort of soup is most commonly served as a first course during Ramadan, but it really is hearty enough to stand as a meal in its own right, especially if served with bread and a salad. The name of this dish literally means "lentils with something sour;" the "something sour" here is lemon, which adds a pleasant tart flavor.

Serves *4 as a first course or 2 as a meal*
Preparation Time: *10 minutes*
Cooking Time: *40 minutes*

1 cup (200 g) dried brown lentils
5 cups (1.25 liters) water
4 tablespoons olive oil
1 large onion, diced
5 large cloves garlic, crushed
½ bunch fresh coriander leaves (cilantro), minced
1 lb (500 g) Swiss chard, stems removed and leaves chopped
2 chicken-flavored soft bouillon cubes
¼ teaspoon salt
⅛ teaspoon freshly ground black pepper
4 tablespoons fresh lemon juice
1 lemon, wedged (for serving)

1 Sort through the lentils to remove any small stones or pieces of dirt, and then rinse with cold water in a colander. Bring the rinsed lentils and the water up to a boil in a lidded medium saucepan. Cover the saucepan, turn the heat down to a simmer, and cook until the lentils are tender, about 20 to 30 minutes, stirring occasionally.
2 While the lentils cook, heat the oil in a medium skillet over medium heat; add the onion and cook until softened, about 5 to 7 minutes, stirring occasionally. Add the garlic and fresh coriander leaves and cook 1 minute more, stirring constantly, then set aside.
3 Once the lentils are tender add the Swiss chard, bouillon cubes, salt and pepper. Turn the heat up to medium, cover the saucepan, and cook until the chard is tender, about 5 to 7 minutes, stirring occasionally. Stir in the onion mixture and cook uncovered until the soup is thickened, about 5 minutes; turn off the heat and stir in the lemon juice.
4 Serve with the lemon wedges to squeeze on top.

Chicken Kebabs (page 88)

CHAPTER SIX

Chicken and Seafood

Chicken is an affordable source of protein that's enjoyed throughout the Middle East in everything from soups, like the Rice and Vegetable Soup that goes with the Roast Chicken on page 90, to sandwiches, like Spiced Shawarma Chicken Wraps (Shawarma Dajaj) (page 92), to impressive rice dishes [see Rice Pilaf with Spiced Smoked Chicken (Mendy Dajaj) (page 94)]. Seafood, on the other hand, is also a favorite, but is much more expensive, which makes it an extravagant meal that s perfect for serving to guests. Fish and other seafood used to be enjoyed only in coastal areas, but now can be found just about everywhere. Along with the availability of seafood, the recipes for it have spread as well; for example, Fish Pilaf with Caramelized Onion (Sayadieh bil Samek) (page 86) was once only enjoyed by fishermen along the coast of Lebanon and Syria, but is now a well known favorite even in land locked areas such as Damascus. The Gulf States of the Middle East are also known for their seafood delicacies. My mother in law spent a good deal of time living in Kuwait, which borders the Persian Gulf, and has many delicious preparations for seafood. there she learned how to prepare many Kuwati seafood dishes, including Shrimp in Aromatic Tomato Sauce (Makboos Rubian) (page 95).

Fish Pilaf with Caramelized Onion — SAYADIEH BIL SAMEK

Traditionally, this dish was a fisherman's delight. These days, it's no longer confined to coastal areas, but is enjoyed all over the Middle East.

5 tablespoons oil, divided
4 tablespoons pine nuts
1 large onion, thinly sliced
3 tablespoons all-purpose flour
1 teaspoon Fish Spice Mix (page 87)
1 teaspoon salt, divided
¾ teaspoon ground cumin, divided
¾ teaspoon ground coriander, divided
¼ teaspoon freshly ground black pepper, divided
1 lb (500 g) medium-textured, mild-flavored white fish fillets (such as cod or haddock), rinsed and patted dry
1 teaspoon Nine Spice Mix (page 29)
½ teaspoon ground turmeric
1½ cups (325 g) uncooked basmati rice
2-2½ cups (500-625 ml) low-sodium fish or chicken stock, boiling
Fresh lemon wedges (for serving)
Chopped Salad with Sesame Dressing (page 47)

Serves *4*
Preparation Time: *20 minutes*
Cooking Time: *45 minutes, plus 15 minutes to let the rice sit after cooking*

1 Prepare Fish Spice Mix and Nine Spice Mix.
2 Heat 4 tablespoons of oil in a large skillet over medium heat. Add the pine nuts and cook until golden brown, about 1 to 2 minutes, stirring constantly. Transfer the pine nuts to a small bowl and set aside.
3 Combine the flour, Fish Spice Mix, ¼ teaspoon salt, ¼ teaspoon cumin, ¼ teaspoon coriander, and ⅛ teaspoon black pepper in a shallow bowl. Dredge the fish in the flour mixture, shaking off the excess. Heat the oil that you cooked the pine nuts in over moderately high heat; add the fish and fry until golden on both sides, about 4 minutes, flipping once. Transfer the fish to a plate (remove the skin, if desired). Cut into large chunks and set aside.
4 With the heat over moderately high, add the onion to the oil that the fish was fried in, and sauté until deep caramel in color, about 15 minutes, stirring occasionally and adding a splash of water as necessary if the onion starts to get too dark. Transfer the onions to a small bowl and set aside.
5 Soak the rice in water for 10 minutes; drain. While the rice is soaking, bring the stock up to a boil. Combine the drained rice with the remaining ¾ teaspoon salt, remaining ¾ teaspoon cumin, remaining ¾ teaspoon coriander, remaining ⅛ teaspoon black pepper, Nine Spice Mix, and turmeric in a large bowl.
6 To layer the rice, drizzle the remaining 1 tablespoon of oil on the bottom of a medium, thick-bottomed, lidded saucepan. Sprinkle ⅓ of the rice across the bottom of the saucepan and arrange ⅓ of the caramelized onion on top; arrange the fish on top in an even layer, then add another ⅓ of the caramelized onion (reserve the remaining ⅓ of the caramelized onion for garnish). Spread the rest of the rice in an even layer on top.
7 Boil the stock and add it to the rice so it's just covered with liquid, about 2 to 2½ cups (500 to 625 ml). Bring to a boil over moderately-high heat, then cover the pot, turn heat down to low, and simmer until the rice is tender, about 12 to 15 minutes, adding a splash of water if necessary. Turn the heat off and let the rice sit (covered) 15 minutes, then fluff with a fork.
8 Transfer to a serving dish and sprinkle the reserved ⅓ of the caramelized onion and the toasted pine nuts on top. Serve with fresh lemon wedges and Chopped Salad with Sesame Dressing.

~Aromatic Whole Roasted Fish~

SAMEK MESHWI

My mother-in-law makes this dish with a kind of fish called *hamour*, which translates to "greasy grouper." Where I live, this kind of fish isn't readily available so instead I use rainbow trout, grouper, or red snapper; you can use any kind of whole fish that's available to you.

If you prefer, instead of using four smaller fish you can use one large fish (about four pounds/two kilograms), just be sure to increase the cooking time (the fish is done when it is opaque and flakes easily with a fork).

Fresh fish is always best, but if it you're using frozen, there is a way to freshen it a bit. In a large bowl, combine ¼ cup (65 ml) fresh lemon juice, ¼ cup (65 ml) apple cider vinegar, and 4 cups (1 liter) cold water. Add the fish and let it soak 10 minutes, then rinse the fish, pat it try, and proceed with the recipe.

Serves *4*
Preparation Time: *25 minutes*
Cooking Time: *30 minutes*

Four (¾-1 lb/350-500 g) whole fish, cleaned head and
   tail intact
1 small and 2 large onions, thinly sliced and divided
5 cloves garlic, minced, divided
2 tablespoons Fish Spice Mix
1 tablespoon ground coriander
1 tablespoon ground cumin
1 teaspoon salt, divided
¼ teaspoon freshly ground black pepper
4 tablespoons apple cider vinegar, divided
4 tablespoons lemon juice
6 tablespoons oil, divided
5 tablespoons water, divided
1 portion Sesame Sauce (page 25)

Fish Spice Mix (Combine the following spices)
1 tablespoon ground black pepper
2 teaspoons ground coriander
2 teaspoons ground ginger
1 teaspoon ground cinnamon
1 teaspoon ground cardamom
1 teaspoon ground nutmeg

1 Rinse the fish and toss it with the small onion, ⅔ of the garlic, Fish Spice Mix, coriander, cumin, ½ teaspoon salt, ¼ teaspoon black pepper, 2 tablespoons vinegar, and lemon juice in a large bowl. Use your hands to rub the spices onto the outside and into the cavity of the fish; let it marinade 10 to 15 minutes.
2 Preheat oven to 450°F (230°C). Add 4 tablespoons of oil to a large skillet over moderately-high heat; add the 2 large onions and ¼ teaspoon salt and sauté until starting to wilt, about 3 to 5 minutes. Transfer the onions to a roasting pan.
3 Combine the remaining ⅓ of the crushed garlic and 3 tablespoons water in a small bowl; set aside.
4 Use your hands to scrape the onion, garlic, and excess spices off the fish, pat it dry, then lay it on top of the onion in the roasting pan. Stir together the remaining ¼ teaspoon salt, 2 tablespoons vinegar, remaining 2 tablespoons oil, and remaining 2 tablespoons water; pour this on top of the fish.
5 Bake 20 minutes, then pour the garlic water over the fish. Continue roasting until the fish is fully cooked, about 5 to 10 minutes more. (When it's done, the fish will be golden outside with opaque flesh that flakes easily with a fork.)
6 Serve immediately, with Sesame Sauce alongside to spoon on top.

Chicken Kebabs

KEBAB DAJAJ

This recipe is perfect for people who love grilled kebabs but aren't big fans of red meat. If you can't find ground chicken, you can easily make your own by grinding boneless, skinless chicken breasts in a meat grinder or food processor.

Serves *4*
Preparation Time: *15 minutes, plus 30 minutes to chill the chicken*
Cooking Time: *10 minutes*

1½ lb (750 g) ground chicken
1 small onion, grated
2 cloves garlic, crushed in a mortar and pestle with
    1 teaspoon salt
1 tablespoon fresh lemon juice
2 tablespoons oil
2 teaspoons Chicken Spice Mix (page 29)
¼ bunch fresh parsley leaves, trim the stems and mince the leaves

1 Prepare Chicken Spice Mix.
2 Use your hands to combine all ingredients in a large bowl.
3 Cover the bowl with plastic wrap and refrigerate until fully chilled, about 30 minutes.
4 Fill a small bowl with water for wetting your hands in between shaping the kebabs. Wet your hands and roll a small handful of the meat mixture into a ball (about the size of an egg), then slide it onto a metal skewer. Flatten the ball so the meat spreads out on the skewer, and repeat this process until all the meat is skewered.
5 Grill until fully cooked, about 10 minutes, flipping once.

Marinated Chicken Skewers

SHEESH TAOUK

Sheesh Taouk is an incredibly flavorful dish with relatively minimal effort. In Damascus it can be bought pre-marinated from just about any butcher and so it is quite a common meal. If you don't have a grill, this chicken can also be skewered, cooked in the oven, and then browned briefly under a broiler. If you want to forgo the skewering altogether, you can cook it on the stovetop in a large skillet with a little oil and some sliced onion. Cooked this way, it is makes a fantastic sandwich filling with some Garlic Mayonnaise (page 24).

Serves *4*
Preparation Time: *15 minutes, plus 1 to 4 hours for the chicken to marinade*
Cooking Time: *10 minutes*

4 tablespoons plain yogurt
2 tablespoons fresh lemon juice
2 tablespoons oil
2 tablespoons tomato paste (optional)
3 cloves garlic, crushed in a mortar and pestle with
    ½ teaspoon salt
2 teaspoons ground paprika
¼ teaspoon ground red pepper (cayenne) (optional)
¼ teaspoon ground allspice
¼ teaspoon freshly ground black pepper
1½ lb (750 g) boneless, skinless chicken breasts,
    trimmed of fat and cut into large cubes

1 Combine the yogurt, lemon juice, oil, tomato paste (if using), garlic, paprika, cayenne (if using), allspice, and black pepper in a medium bowl. Add the chicken and toss to coat; refrigerate at least 1 hour but up to 4 hours.
2 Use your hands to remove any excess marinade from the chicken pieces and thread the chicken onto skewers.
3 Grill until fully cooked, about 10 minutes, flipping once halfway through.

Roasted Green Wheat with Chicken

FREEKEH BIL DAJAJ

Freekeh is an extremely healthy whole grain with a smoky, nutty flavor. For more information on *Freekeh*, see Roasted Green Wheat (Freekeh) (page 22).

Serves *4*
Preparation Time: *10 minutes, plus 30 minutes to soak the wheat*
Cooking Time: *40 minutes, plus 10 minutes to let the wheat sit after cooking*

1¼ cups (175 g) roasted green wheat
3 tablespoons clarified butter (or 1 tablespoon unsalted butter and 1 tablespoon canola oil)
2 tablespoons pine nuts or blanched almonds
1 onion, finely diced
1½ teaspoons Nine Spice Mix (page 29), divided
2 bay leaves
1¼ teaspoons salt, divided
2¼ cups (565 ml) low-sodium chicken broth or water
2 tablespoons olive oil
1 lb (500 g) boneless, skinless chicken breast, sliced crosswise into ½-inch (1.25 cm) thick slices
Plain yogurt (optional, for serving)

1 Prepare Nine Spice Mix.
2 Sort through the wheat to remove any irregular pieces, small stones, or pieces of dirt, and then rinse with cold water in a colander. Soak the wheat in cold water for 30 minutes, skimming off any debris that rises to the surface and changing the water two or three times; drain.
3 Add the butter to a medium, thick-bottomed lidded saucepan over medium heat. Add the nuts and cook until golden brown, about 1 to 2 minutes, stirring constantly. Use a slotted spoon to transfer the pine nuts to a small bowl; set aside.
4 Boil the chicken broth or water.
5 Add the onion to the saucepan you cooked the nuts in, and cook until softened and just starting to brown, about 5 to 7 minutes, stirring occasionally. Add the wheat, 1 teaspoon Nine Spice Mix, bay leaves, and 1 teaspoon salt, and cook 2 minutes, stirring frequently. Pour the boiled broth or water into the saucepan, stirring. Turn the heat up to high, and bring to a rolling boil.
6 Give the wheat a stir, then cover the saucepan, turn the heat down to low, and cook until tender, about 20 to 30 minutes; the water should be mostly absorbed but the wheat should still be slightly moist. Once it's done cooking, let it sit with the lid on for 10 minutes, then fluff with a fork.
7 While the wheat cooks, cook the chicken. Sprinkle the remaining ½ teaspoon Nine Spice Mix and the remaining ¼ teaspoon salt onto the chicken. Heat the oil in a large skillet over moderately high heat; add the chicken and sauté until fully cooked and lightly browned on both sides, about 4 to 5 minutes.
8 To serve, transfer the wheat to a large platter or bowl; arrange the chicken on top and then sprinkle on the pine nuts. Serve immediately, with plain yogurt.

Roast Chicken with Rice and Vegetable Soup

MOLOKHIA NA'AMEH

The name of this soup means "for royalty" and it has quite the royal history, as it originated in ancient Egypt and was food for the nobles. Now it is one of Egypt's national dishes and is commonly eaten across the Middle East. It is made of minced jute mallow leaves; you can mince your own fresh leaves if they're available. A mincing knife is the perfect tool for this job (see page 16 for more information), but if it isn't available fresh, frozen minced jute mallow is commonly found in Middle Eastern grocery stores. (Dried minced jute mallow can also be found, but I find that the flavor of frozen is preferable to dried.)

Once cooked, this soup is thick with a slimy consistency, very similar to cooked okra. The flavor is a bit like spinach, but earthier somehow. It can also be made with lamb or beef stew meat instead of chicken, if you prefer. For more flavor, sauté ¼ bunch minced fresh coriander leaves or 2 teaspoons ground coriander along with the garlic.

Serves *4*
Preparation Time: *15 minutes*
Cooking Time: *55 minutes*

1 whole chicken, with the innards, giblets, head,
   and neck removed
2 tablespoons olive oil, divided
1 teaspoon salt, divided
¼ teaspoon black pepper, divided
2 cups (500 ml) water
1 chicken-flavored soft bouillon cube
1 bay leaf
1 small onion, peeled and quartered
1 (14 oz/400 g) bag frozen minced jute mallow
2 cloves garlic, crushed in a mortar and pestle
1 lemon, wedged (for serving)
1 batch Rice with Toasted Vermicelli
   Noodles (page 58) for serving

1 Prepare the Rice with Toasted Vermicelli Noodles.
2 Cut out the chicken's backbone; quarter the chicken so you have 2 breasts and 2 thigh/leg pieces, and then cut each breast into 2 pieces, leaving the wing attached (you will end up with 6 pieces total; if you prefer, you can also separate the leg and thigh so you end up with 8 pieces total). Cut away the wing tips and excess fat, leaving the skin on. Rinse and pat the chicken dry.
3 Preheat the oven to 350°F (175°C). Arrange the chicken in a single layer on a large baking sheet; drizzle 1 tablespoon oil on top; sprinkle on ½ teaspoon salt and ⅛ teaspoon black pepper. Roast until the juices run clear when poked with a sharp knife, about 50 to 60 minutes. Once roasted, if you want the chicken to have more color, you can broil it for a couple of minutes.
4 While the chicken cooks, prepare the jute mallow. Add the water, bouillon cube, bay leaf, onion, remaining ½ teaspoon salt, and remaining ⅛ teaspoon black pepper to a medium saucepan.
5 Bring to a boil, then stir in the jute mallow; let the soup come back up to a boil and then turn the heat down to a simmer. If the jute mallow is still frozen, simmer 10 to 15 minutes; if it is partially or fully thawed, simmer 7 minutes.
6 Add the remaining 1 tablespoon of oil and the garlic to a small skillet over medium-low heat; cook until fragrant, 45 to 60 seconds, stirring constantly. Stir the garlic into the soup.
7 Serve the soup and chicken with lemon and Rice with Toasted Vermicelli Noodles.

Spiced Shawarma Chicken Wraps

SHAWARMA DAJAJ

Shawarma is the Middle East's version of fast food, and in populated areas you probably won't walk a block without seeing half a dozen or so shawarma vendors. Shawarma is made from chicken, lamb, or beef (or occasionally other meats like goat) that has been marinated, wrapped around a stick, and cooked on a vertical rotisserie; the meat is then shaved off and made into sandwiches. Not many of us (including me) have a vertical rotisserie, so when my husband and I were first married and he moved from the Middle East to the U.S., I had to find another way to make his favorite fast food that still tastes like the real deal without the use of this piece of equipment. I use a two-step cooking process—roasting in the oven, followed by sautéing on the stovetop—which results in delicious and authentic-tasting shawarma.

Once the meat is cooked you can either serve it in a shallow dish to scoop up with flatbread, or roll it into sandwiches. If you make it into sandwiches, you can add just about any vegetables you like (such as lettuce, cucumber, tomato, and/or onion), but no matter what you add, there are two components that need to be present: pickles and creamy garlic sauce. The garlic sauce (called *Toumieh*) is really more of a garlic-y mayonnaise, and my opinion it makes the shawarma.

Once the chicken is roasted, it can be stored in the fridge for up to three days before being sautéed, which makes it perfect for leftovers.

Serves *8*
Preparation Time: *30 minutes, plus 2 to 24 hours for the chicken to marinate*
Cooking Time: *1 hour, 15 minutes*

1 batch Shawarma Spice Mix
½ cup (125 ml) plain yogurt
1½ tablespoons fresh lemon juice
3 large cloves garlic, crushed
1½ teaspoons salt
2 lb (1 kg) boneless, skinless chicken breast
2 tablespoons olive oil, plus more for sautéing
16 flatbreads
Garlic Mayonnaise (page 24)
Pickles (page 27)

Shawarma Spice Mix
2 teaspoons ground cumin
2 teaspoons ground coriander
¾ teaspoon ground black pepper
½ teaspoon ground ginger
½ teaspoon ground allspice
¼ teaspoon ground fenugreek
¼ teaspoon ground cardamom
¼ teaspoon ground cloves
¼ teaspoon ground sweet paprika
¼ teaspoon ground turmeric
⅛ teaspoon ground red pepper (cayenne) (optional)

1 Prepare the Shawarma Spice Mix.
2 Combine the spice mix with the yogurt, lemon juice, garlic, and salt in a large bowl. Add the chicken and toss to coat. Cover and refrigerate 2 to 24 hours.
3 Preheat oven to 350°F and spread 1 tablespoon of oil on the inside of a large baking dish.
4 Scrape off any excess marinade from the chicken with your hands. Starting in the center of the oiled dish, arrange the chicken so that it overlaps, and drizzle the remaining 1 tablespoon of oil on top. Bake (uncovered) 1 hour, or until the chicken is fully cooked; cool. (It's done when you cut into the center and there is no pink.)
5 Remove the chicken from the pan and transfer it to a large cutting board; slice it very thinly across the grain, then transfer it back into the pan it was cooked in to soak up the juices (the chicken can be refrigerated this way for up to 3 days before continuing with the rest of the recipe, or you can continue after 10 minutes).
6 Coat the bottom of a large skillet over medium-high heat with oil. Once hot, add the sliced chicken and sauté until crispy and golden brown (you may need to sauté the chicken in two or three batches so the pan isn't overcrowded).
7 Spread some Garlic Mayonnaise in the center of each piece of bread; add some chicken and pickles (and any other vegetables you like) and roll it up.
8 Toast the sandwiches on a dry griddle or a flat sandwich press so that the bread gets golden brown and slightly crispy.
9 Serve as is, or cut into small rounds; serve with additional Garlic Mayonnaise for dipping.

Rice Pilaf with Spiced Smoked Chicken

MENDY DAJAJ

This is a Saudi dish that's commonly eaten all over the Gulf States. The chicken is traditionally smoked underground; however, my mother-in-law came up with a brilliant smoking method that can be done right in your kitchen. While the smoking method is my mother-in-law's, credit for teaching me this recipe goes to my brother-in-law, who worked as a chef in Dubai for a while.

Serves *4 to 6*
Preparation Time: *15 minutes*
Cooking Time: *55 minutes, plus 15 minutes to smoke the chicken and rice*

4 tablespoons plain yogurt
1 tablespoon olive oil
1 tablespoon Mendy Spice Mix (page 29)
½ teaspoon salt
1 whole fresh chicken, cut into serving pieces

For Smoky Flavor
1 tablespoon olive oil
1 piece of charcoal

For Serving
2 cups (500 g) plain yogurt
Fresh Tomato Sauce (page 53)

Rice Pilaf
1½ cups (325 g) uncooked basmati rice
2 tablespoons clarified butter
  (or 1 tablespoon unsalted butter plus 1 tablespoon canola oil)
4 tablespoons cashews or blanched almonds
1 onion, finely diced
1¾ cups (425 ml) water or chicken stock
1 chicken-flavored soft bouillon cube
2 bay leaves
2 dried limes (*loomi*), pierced with a paring knife a couple times
One 2 in (5 cm) cinnamon stick
½ tablespoon whole green cardamom pods, cracked
½ teaspoon whole cloves
½ whole nutmeg
¼ teaspoon whole peppercorns

1 Prepare Mendy Spice Mix and Fresh Tomato Sauce.

2 Preheat oven to 350°F (175°C). Combine the yogurt, olive oil, Mendy Spice Mix, and salt in a small bowl and set aside.

3 Place the chicken in a large bowl, add the yogurt mixture, and rub the yogurt into each piece of chicken. (If there is time, cover the chicken and let it marinade in the fridge for up to 4 hours.)

4 Use your hands to scrape off any excess yogurt and arrange the chicken in a single layer on a large baking sheet. Roast until the juices run clear when poked with a sharp knife, about 50 to 60 minutes.

5 While the chicken roasts, soak the rice in water for 10 minutes; drain. While the rice is soaking, bring the water, and added spices to a boil in a medium saucepan over medium heat.

6 Add the clarified butter to a thick-bottomed lidded saucepan over medium heat. Add the cashews and cook until golden brown, about 2 minutes, stirring constantly. Transfer to a small bowl and set aside.

7 Add the onion to the saucepan you cooked the nuts in, and cook until softened and just starting to brown, about 3 to 5 minutes, stirring occasionally. Add the rice and cook 2 minutes, stirring frequently. Add the boiling water (with all the spices), turn the heat up to high, and bring to a rolling boil.

8 Give the rice a stir, then cover, turn the heat down to very low, and cook until tender, about 10 minutes (do not open the lid during this time). Turn the heat off and let the rice sit 15 minutes, then fluff with a fork.

9 Place the chicken on top of the rice (or if the pot isn't big enough, transfer both the rice and the chicken to a large lidded casserole pot that's large enough to hold them both); nestle a heat-safe cup or bowl in the center and pour the olive oil into the cup. Heat the piece of charcoal until glowing red, then use tongs to place it in the cup with the oil. Immediately cover the pot and let it smoke for 15 minutes.

10 Carefully remove the dish of oil and transfer the rice to a large serving platter; top with the chicken and sprinkle on the cashews. Serve with plain yogurt and Fresh Tomato Sauce to spoon on top.

Shrimp in Aromatic Tomato Sauce

MAKBOOS RUBIAN

This is a classic dish from the Gulf area that my mother-in-law learned when she lived there during the '80's. It's usually served with beautiful, aromatic Saffron Rice with Golden Raisins and Pine Nuts (page 61).

Serves *4*
Preparation Time: *5 minutes*
Cooking Time: *30 minutes*

1-1½ lb (750 g) fresh large shrimp, peeled and
   deveined (about 36-40 shrimp per pound)
3 tablespoons olive oil, divided
1 large onion, halved and thinly sliced
2 cloves garlic, crushed in a mortar and pestle with
   ¾ teaspoon salt
3 tomatoes, peeled and diced
2 tablespoons tomato paste
1 cup (250 ml) water
1 bay leaf
3 pods cardamom, crushed
2 whole cloves
1 teaspoon ground cumin
½ teaspoon ground coriander
½ teaspoon ground turmeric
½ teaspoon ground cinnamon
½ teaspoon ground paprika
½ teaspoon ground red pepper (cayenne)
¼ teaspoon freshly ground nutmeg
¼ teaspoon ground allspice
¼ teaspoon freshly ground black pepper
1 portion Saffron Rice with Golden Raisins and
   Pine Nuts, for serving (page 61)

1 Prepare the Saffron Rice with Golden Raisins and Pine Nuts.
2 Heat 2 tablespoons of oil in a large lidded skillet over medium heat; add the onion and cook until softened, about 5 to 7 minutes, stirring occasionally. Add the garlic and tomato and cook 2 minutes, then add the tomato paste and water and bring up to a boil. Cover the skillet, turn the heat down to simmer, and cook 10 minutes, stirring occasionally.

3 Heat the remaining 1 tablespoon of oil in a medium skillet over medium heat; add the shrimp, bay leaf, cardamom, cloves, cumin, ground coriander, turmeric, cinnamon ground sweet paprika, ground red pepper, nutmeg, allspice, and black pepper. Cook until the shrimp turns pink (about 2 to 3 minutes).
4 Stir the shrimp mixture into the tomato sauce and serve immediately with Saffron Rice with Raisins and Pine Nuts.

Baked Chicken with Red Rice Pilaf

KEBSEH

This classic Saudi dish is an impressive sight to see; it's usually brought steaming hot out to the table on a huge serving platter with the colorful rice on the bottom, the meat on top, and nuts interspersed. It's the perfect meal for a special celebration, or when you want to impress your guests. (*Note:* Lamb or beef can be used instead of the chicken if you prefer.)

Serves *4 to 6*
Preparation Time: *40 minutes*
Cooking Time: *55 minutes, plus 15 minutes to let the rice sit after cooking*

1 whole fresh chicken, cut into serving pieces
1 tablespoon plain yogurt
4 tablespoons olive oil
1¼ teaspoons salt
2 teaspoons Kebseh Spice Mix (page 29), divided
1 tablespoon canola oil
1 small onion, finely diced
1 small green bell pepper, deseeded and finely diced
1 small tomato, peeled and finely diced
2 large cloves garlic, minced
1½ tablespoons tomato paste
1½ cups (325 g) uncooked basmati rice
1¾ cups (425 ml) boiling water
4 tablespoons pine nuts or blanched almonds

1 Prepare Kebseh Spice Mix.
2 Combine the yogurt, 1 tablespoon olive oil, ½ teaspoon salt, and 1 teaspoon of Kebseh Spice Mix in a large bowl. Add the chicken and toss gently to coat.
3 Preheat the oven to 350°F (175°C). Arrange the chicken in a single layer on a large baking sheet. Roast until the juices run clear when poked with a sharp knife, about 50 to 60 minutes. Once roasted, if you want the chicken to have more color, you can broil it for a couple minutes.
4 Heat 1 tablespoon of olive oil and the canola oil in a medium saucepan over moderately-high heat; add the onion and green bell pepper and sauté until completely softened, about 12 to 15 minutes, stirring occasionally. Add the diced tomato and garlic and cook until the tomato is completely soft, about 5 to 7 minutes, stirring occasionally. Stir in the tomato paste, turn the heat down to medium, and cook until the sauce is thickened, about 3 minutes.

5 Soak the rice in water for 10 minutes; drain. While the rice is soaking, put half a kettle of water on to boil.
6 Add the remaining 2 tablespoons of olive oil to a medium, thick-bottomed lidded saucepan over medium heat. Add the pine nuts and cook until golden brown, about 1 to 2 minutes, stirring constantly. Transfer to a small bowl and set aside.
7 Add the rice to the saucepan you cooked the pine nuts in, turn heat up to high, and cook 2 minutes, stirring frequently. Stir in the tomato mixture, boiling water, remaining 1 teaspoon Kebseh Spice Mix, and remaining ¾ teaspoon salt and bring to a rolling boil.
8 Give the rice a stir, then cover the saucepan, turn the heat down to very low, and cook until tender, about 10 minutes (do not open the lid during this time). Turn the heat off and let the rice sit (covered) 15 minutes, then fluff with a fork.
9 Transfer to a serving dish, arrange the chicken pieces on top, and sprinkle on the toasted pine nuts; serve.

Roasted Chicken with Flatbread

M'SAKHKHAN

Although it's popular all over the Middle East, this dish is Palestinian in origin. Traditionally, it's made with a thick and chewy, blistered bread, called *Taboon*. It's always impressive to see a tray of *M'sakhkhan* brought out, but it's actually a fairly simple dish that's mainly about good quality olive oil, chicken, and sumac, which gives the dish a pleasant sour tang.

Like so many Middle Eastern dishes, this one has numerous variations; no matter which variation you make, the chicken and onions are typically wrapped in bread and eaten with your hands.

If you have leftover chicken on hand, you can make a quick version of this dish. Shred the chicken and sauté some onion in olive oil with sumac. Add the chicken to the onion and roll the onion/chicken mixture up as sandwiches in flatbread. Arrange the sandwiches in a baking dish, drizzle the tops with a little olive oil, and broil until golden brown and crispy.

Serves *4 to 6*
Preparation Time: *30 minutes*
Cooking Time: *2 hours*

1 large fresh chicken, cut into serving pieces
1 teaspoon salt, divided
¾ cup (175 ml) olive oil, divided
4 lb (2 kg) onions, halved and thinly sliced
5 tablespoons sumac, divided
½ teaspoon ground allspice
¼ teaspoon freshly ground black pepper
3 pieces *taboon* bread, or 3-6 large pita breads or
    Middle Eastern flatbreads
1 tablespoon clarified butter (or ½ tablespoon
    unsalted butter plus ½ tablespoon canola oil)
4 tablespoons pine nuts

1 Whisk together 1 tablespoon of oil and 1 tablespoon of sumac in a small bowl; set aside. Transfer 4 tablespoons oil to a large pot over high heat. Add chicken and brown on both sides, about 4 minutes per side. Transfer the chicken to a plate and set aside.
2 Turn the heat down to medium and add the onion and remaining 3 tablespoons of oil. Cook until the onions are softened and translucent, about 30 minutes, stirring occasionally. Stir in 4 tablespoons sumac, allspice, black pepper, and the remaining ½ teaspoon salt and cook 3 minutes more, stirring frequently.
3 Preheat oven to 350°F (175°C). Place 1 piece of bread on the bottom of a large, round oven-safe tray (if you don't have a tray that's large enough to fit the taboon bread, you can break the bread into smaller pieces and arrange it in a single layer). Top the bread with ⅓ of the cooked onion mixture; top the onions with another piece of bread (or a layer of broken bread), then top the bread with another ⅓ of the onion mixture. Place the last piece of bread on top and top with the last ⅓ of the onion mixture. Arrange the chicken on top of the bread and sprinkle on the oil/sumac mixture. Bake (uncovered) until the chicken is fully cooked, about 1 hour to 1½ hours.
4 While the chicken bakes, toast the pine nuts. Melt the clarified butter in a small saucepan over low heat; add the pine nuts and cook until light golden brown, about 2 minutes, stirring constantly.
5 When the chicken is out of the oven, sprinkle the pine nuts on top and serve.

Lamb and Navy Bean Soup
(page 108)

CHAPTER SEVEN

Beef and Lamb

Beef is eaten in the Middle East, but lamb is generally the preferred red meat; however, in the recipes in this book you can use beef and lamb interchangeably to suit your preferences. Along with the dishes in Chapter 7 (Chicken and Seafood), many recipes contained in this section are for more formal meals, the kinds of meals that are used for entertaining guests. For a guest whom you particularly like or want to show your generosity, you either buy several different kinds of meat and grill everything, see Lamb or Beef Kebab (Kebab wa Kufta) (page 112), or you make some kind of stuffed vegetables, see Stuffed Marrow Squash in Yogurt Sauce (Kousa Mahshi bil Leban) (page 104) and Stuffed Marrow Squash (Kousa Mahshi) (page 107). However, some of the recipes in this section are less formal, and are perfect for using up a small amount of leftover meat, such as Meat Sautéed with Leeks (Bellassia) (page 106) and Scrambled Eggs with Meat and Onion (Bayd bil Lahmeh wa Bussel) (page 105).

Kibbeh with Variations — LAMB AND BULGUR WHEAT

Kibbeh is found all over the Middle East and there are dozens of different variations. It can be shaped into just about any form you can imagine and then fried, grilled, boiled, or baked. Some versions are stuffed and other recipes have accompanying sauces. Perhaps the most commonly known form of Kibbeh is fried; these fritters are filled with stuffing (typically meat) and are known by their signature shape: a slightly elongated sphere with pointed ends (like an American football or a torpedo). Because this dish is time-consuming and a bit more difficult to make than most, it's what you make for guests you want to impress.

Fried Kibbeh may be difficult to shape at first, but as you practice you will get much faster and more adept at it. (I didn't grow up making Kibbeh and I don't make it very often, so when I do make it, I can always see which ones I made at the beginning of the batch and which ones I made later…you really will improve that quickly at making these!)

Note: Beef can be used instead of lamb in any Kibbeh recipe. The meat should be very lean (such as from the loin) with no tendons or sinew; also, it must be very fresh and very, very finely ground.

VARIATION 1
Fried Kibbeh
KIBBEH MEKLIYEH

Yields *about 45 pieces*
Preparation Time: *2 hours, 30 minutes*
Cooking Time: *1 hour*

1 lb (500 g) finely ground bulgur wheat
Water, to soak the bulgur
1 tablespoon salt
1 teaspoon ground cumin
1 teaspoon ground coriander
¼ teaspoon ground black pepper
1 onion, peeled and quartered
½ lb (250 g) lean lamb, very finely ground
4-6 tablespoons water, to moisten the dough
Oil, for deep-frying
Salad and/or plain yogurt (optional, for serving)

Filling
1½ tablespoons oil
One large onion, finely diced
¾ teaspoons salt, divided
¾ lb (350 g) lean lamb, very finely ground
½ teaspoon Syrian Spice Mix (page 29)
½ teaspoon ground cumin
½ teaspoon ground coriander
¼ teaspoon ground black pepper
2 tablespoons pine nuts

1 Prepare Syrian Spice Mix.

2 To make the filling, add the oil to a large skillet over medium heat; once hot, add the onion and ¼ teaspoon salt and fry until softened, about 7 minutes, stirring occasionally. Add the ground lamb, remaining ½ teaspoon salt, Syrian Spice Mix, cumin, coriander, and black pepper. Cook until browned, about 5 minutes, stirring occasionally and using a wooden spoon to break up the meat. Stir in the pine nuts and cook 3 minutes more, stirring occasionally. Taste and season with additional salt and pepper as desired; cool completely.

3 Pour the bulgur into the bottom of a large bowl and fill the rest of the bowl with tepid water; soak 15 minutes and then drain out the water.

4 Mix the bulgur with the salt, cumin, coriander, and black pepper. Grind the bulgur and onion in a meat grinder (fine grind), a stand mixer fitted with a food grinding attachment (fine grind), or in a heavy-duty food processor until it feels very soft (it takes 2 to 3 times using a meat grinder or stand mixer fitted with a food grinding attachment). Transfer the bulgur mixture to a large bowl and use your hands to knead in the meat; as you're kneading, add water (about 4-6 tablespoons) so that the mixture comes together to form a dough.

5 To stuff the Kibbeh, have a bowl of room temperature water nearby for wetting your hands. Wet your hands, then scoop out 2 tablespoons of the bulgur mixture and shape it into an oval. Put a finger into one end, then while turning the oval with one hand, keep your finger from the other hand still so that it acts like a drill and the opening gets

bigger. Stuff about 2 teaspoons of the meat filling into the opening, then wet your fingers and gently pinch the bulgur together to close the opening; shape both ends so they're slightly pointed. Continue this way with the rest of the bulgur mixture and filling.

6 Fill a large, heavy-bottomed pot halfway full with oil; warm over medium-high heat until it reaches 350°F (175°C). Fry the Kibbeh in batches so the pot isn't overcrowded; cook each batch until the Kibbeh is golden brown (about 4 to 6 minutes per batch). Transfer the cooked Kibbeh to a paper towel-lined plate to drain any excess oil.

7 Serve hot, warm, or room temperature with salad and/or plain yogurt, if desired.

VARIATION 2
Fried Kibbeh in Yogurt Sauce

KIBBEH LABANIYEH

Serves *8*
Preparation Time: *2 hours, 30 minutes*
Cooking Time: *1 hour, 15 minutes*

1 batch Fried Kibbeh (above)
2 batches Yogurt Sauce, prepared with dried, crushed tarragon (see Meat-Stuffed Marrow Squash in Yogurt Sauce (Kousa Mahshi bil Leban) and its headnote (page 104))

Prepare the fried Kibbeh and add to the yogurt sauce, turn heat down to low, and cook until warm, about 3 minutes.

Forming the Kibbeh

STEP 1: Scoop out two tablespoons of the bulgur mixture.

STEP 2: Shape the bulgur into an oval by rolling it between your hands; put a finger into one end, then while turning the oval with one hand, keep your finger from the other hand still so that it acts like a drill and the opening gets bigger.

STEP 3: Stuff about 2 teaspoons of the meat filling into the opening, then wet your fingers and gently pinch the bulgur together to close the opening.

STEP 4: Shape both ends so they're slightly pointed.

VARIATION 3
Baked Kibbeh Pies
KIBBEH BIL FURUN

Yields *2 pies (9 in/23 cm)*
Preparation Time: *2 hours, 30 minutes*
Cooking Time: *1 hour, 15 minutes*

1 lb (500 g) finely ground bulgur
    wheat
Water, to soak the bulgur
1 tablespoon salt
1 teaspoon ground cumin
1 teaspoon ground coriander
¼ teaspoon ground black pepper
1 small onion, peeled and quartered
½ lb (250 g) lean lamb, finely ground
4-6 tablespoons water, to moisten the
    dough

Filling
1½ tablespoons canola oil
One large onion, finely diced
¾ teaspoon salt, divided
¾ lb (350 g) lean lamb, finely ground
½ teaspoon Syrian Spice Mix
    (page 29)
½ teaspoon cumin
½ teaspoon coriander
¼ teaspoon black pepper
2 tablespoons pine nuts
½ cup (125 ml) olive oil, divided

1 Prepare the Syrian Spice Mix
2 To make the filling, add the oil to a large skillet over medium heat; once hot, add the onion and ¼ teaspoon salt and fry until softened, about 7 minutes, stirring occasionally. Add the ground lamb, remaining ½ teaspoon salt, Syrian Spice Mix, cumin, coriander, and black pepper. Cook until browned, about 5 to 7 minutes, stirring occasionally and using a wooden spoon to break up the meat. Stir in the pine nuts and cook 3 minutes more, stirring occasionally. Taste and season with additional salt and pepper as desired, cool completely.
3 Pour the bulgur into the bottom of a large bowl and fill the rest of the bowl with tepid water; soak 15 minutes and then drain out the water.
4 Mix the bulgur with the salt, cumin, coriander, and black pepper. Grind the bulgur and onion in a meat grinder (fine grind), a stand mixer fitted with a food grinding attachment (fine grind), or in a heavy-duty food processor until it feels very soft (it takes 2 to 3 times using a meat grinder or stand mixer fitted with a food grinding attachment). Transfer the bulgur mixture to a large bowl and use your hands to knead in the meat; as you're kneading, add water (4-6 tablespoons)so that the mixture comes together to form a dough.
5 Preheat oven to 400°F (200°C); brush 1 tablespoon of olive oil on the bottom and up the sides of 2 baking pans (9-inches/23 cm) . Divide the bulgur mixture into 4 equal parts; roll each into a ball and flatten slightly into a disk. Roll each disk out between 2 pieces of parchment paper to a 9-inch (23 cm) circle.
6 Place 1 circle of dough into the bottom of each prepared pan; wet your hands and smooth the dough into an even layer in the bottom of the pan. Divide the filling between the 2 pans, spreading it out evenly, and leaving a ¼-inch (6 mm) rim all the way around. Place the remaining 2 dough circles on top of the filling in each pan; again, wet your hands and smooth the dough into an even layer, gently pressing it down.
7 Run a knife along the outer rim of the pan, and then score a decorative criss-cross pattern on top. Drizzle 3 tablespoons olive oil on top of each pie. Bake until golden brown along the outer rim, about 30 to 40 minutes. Once cooked, if you want the top of the Kibbeh to have more color, you can broil it for a couple minutes.

VARIATION 4
Raw Kibbeh
KIBBEH NAYEH

Serves *6*
Preparation Time: *35 minutes*
Cooking Time: *0 minutes*

½ lb (250 g) finely ground bulgur wheat
Water, to soak the bulgur
½ tablespoon salt
½ teaspoon ground cumin
½ teaspoon ground coriander
⅛ teaspoon ground black pepper
1 onion, peeled and quartered
½ cup shelled walnuts
½ lb (250 g) lean lamb, very finely ground
2 tablespoons pomegranate molasses
1-2 teaspoons dried red pepper flakes,
    plus more for garnish (optional)
Ice cold water, to moisten the dough
    (about 2 tablespoons)
2 tablespoons olive oil (for garnish)
1 sprig fresh parsley or mint (for garnish)

1 Pour the bulgur into the bottom of a large bowl and fill the rest of the bowl with tepid water; soak 15 minutes and then drain out the water.
2 Mix the bulgur with the salt, cumin, coriander, and black pepper. Grind the bulgur, onion, and walnut in a meat grinder (fine grind), a stand mixer fitted with a food grinding attachment (fine grind), or in a heavy-duty food processor until it feels very soft (it takes 2 to 3 times using a meat grinder or stand mixer fitted with a food grinding attachment).
3 Transfer the bulgur mixture to a large bowl and use your hands to knead in the meat, pomegranate molasses, and dried red pepper flakes; as you're kneading, add water (about 2 tablespoons) so that the mixture comes together to form a dough.
4 Shape the raw Kibbeh into small, finger-shaped pieces or spread it out in a shallow dish. Drizzle the olive oil on top and a sprinkle on the parsley or mint, and a little bit of dried red pepper flakes, if using. Serve immediately.

Meat and Vegetable Casserole with Pomegranate

KOWAJ

The first time I had this dish its flavor completely surprised me; I knew it would be good, but I had no idea it would be this good. *It's the pomegranate molasses.*

Serves *6*
Preparation Time: *20 minutes*
Cooking Time: *1 hour, 20 minutes (1 hour of which is bake time)*

2 tablespoons olive oil
2 onions, diced
1 lb (500 g) lean ground lamb or beef
1¾ teaspoons salt, divided
¼ teaspoon freshly ground black pepper
3 cloves garlic, minced
1 lb (500 g) tomatoes, peeled and diced
1 lb (500 g) potatoes, peeled and cubed
1 lb (500 g) marrow squash, zucchini, or eggplant, cubed (peeled if using eggplant)
2 tablespoons tomato paste
2 tablespoons pomegranate molasses
½ cup (125 ml) water
¼ bunch fresh parsley leaves, minced
Flatbread or Rice with Toasted Vermicelli Noodles (page 58) (for serving)

1 Preheat the oven to 350°F (175°C).
2 Heat the oil in a large skillet over medium heat; add the onion and sauté until starting to soften, about 5 minutes, stirring occasionally. Add the meat, 1 teaspoon salt, and the pepper; turn the heat up to high and cook until the meat is fully browned and the onion is tender, about 5 minutes, stirring occasionally and using a wooden spoon to break up the meat. Add the garlic and tomato and cook 5 minutes more.
3 Transfer the meat mixture to a medium-sized casserole dish along with the potato and marrow squash (or zucchini or eggplant); stir to combine.
4 Whisk together the tomato paste, pomegranate molasses, water, and remaining salt in a small bowl; drizzle on top of the casserole.
5 Cover the casserole dish and bake until the veggies are tender, about 1 hour to 1 hour, 15 minutes.
6 Stir in the fresh parsley leaves and serve with Arabic flatbread or Rice with Toasted Vermicelli Noodles.

Stuffed Squash with Yogurt Sauce

KOUSA MAHSHI BIL LABAN

This dish is a variant of Stuffed Marrow Squash (page 107), but instead of rice as part of the stuffing, it is served on the side. The tomato sauce is replaced with a creamy yogurt sauce that's eaten like a soup or spooned on top of everything.

Leftovers are simple to reheat. Put the zucchini in a separate pot from the yogurt sauce. Add enough hot water to come just below the top of the zucchini, and bring to a simmer over low heat (do not stir); simmer until warm throughout, about three to five minutes. Meanwhile, bring the yogurt sauce up to a simmer in a heavy-bottomed saucepan over low heat, stirring constantly in one direction with a wooden spoon. If the yogurt sauce is too thick, you can add a splash of the water that the zucchini was reheated in to thin it out.

(*Note:* For a more flavorful yogurt sauce, add 1 tablespoon dried, crushed mint or 1 tablespoon dried, crushed tarragon, along with sautéed garlic. To sauté the garlic, add 1 tablespoon canola oil to a small pan over low heat; add 2 cloves of crushed garlic and cook until fragrant and light golden, about 2 to 3 minutes, stirring constantly. Stir the dried tarragon or mint into the garlic and add this mixture to the yogurt sauce before adding the zucchini.)

Serves *4 to 6*
Preparation Time: *1 hour*
Cooking Time: *1 hour, 15 minutes*

Meat-Stuffed Marrow Squash
2 lb (1 kg) marrow squash or small zucchini, hollowed out
   (see Hollowing Out Vegetables to Stuff, page 12)
2 tablespoons oil, divided
2 large onions, diced
1 lb (500 g) lean ground lamb or beef
1 teaspoons salt
1 teaspoon Syrian Spice Mix (page 29)
¼ teaspoon freshly ground black pepper
3 tablespoons pine nuts
Rice with Toasted Vermicelli Noodles (page 58)

Yogurt Sauce
2 lb (1 kg or about 3⅓ cups) plain yogurt, room temperature
1 large egg, lightly beaten
2 tablespoons cornstarch dissolved in 4 tablespoons cold water
½ teaspoon salt

1 Preheat oven to 375°F (190°C); line a baking sheet with parchment paper and brush ½ tablespoon of oil on the paper.
2 Heat the remaining 1½ tablespoons of oil in a large skillet over medium heat; add the onion and sauté until it starts to soften, about 5 minutes, stirring occasionally. Add the ground meat, salt, Syrian Spice Mix, and black pepper; turn heat up to high and cook until the meat is fully browned and the onion is tender, about 5 minutes, stirring occasionally and using a wooden spoon to break up the meat. Stir in the pine nuts and cook 3 minutes more, stirring occasionally. Cool slightly.
3 Stuff the meat mixture into the hollowed out marrow squash/zucchini, packing firmly and leaving about ½ inch (1.25 cm) at the top of each. Transfer to the prepared baking sheet and roll to coat with the oil. Bake until the marrow squash/zucchini is tender and golden in places, about 40 minutes, flipping once halfway through, set aside. (Alternatively, these can be deep fried until golden.)
4 Make the Yogurt Sauce by combining the yogurt, egg, dissolved cornstarch, and remaining salt in a large, heavy-bottomed saucepan over medium heat. Bring to a boil while stirring constantly in one direction with a wooden spoon, then turn the heat down and simmer 2 minutes, continuing to stir constantly.
5 Add the zucchini to the Yogurt Sauce, bring to a simmer over low heat, and simmer uncovered 10 minutes. (If the sauce thickens too much add a splash of water.) To prevent the zucchini from breaking apart, do not stir (it's better to swirl the pot if necessary). Remove the zucchini and strain the Yogurt Sauce to remove any lumps, if desired.
6 To serve, pour the Yogurt Sauce into individual bowls (to be eaten as soup or spooned on top of everything), arrange the zucchini on a platter, and serve alongside Rice with Toasted Vermicelli Noodles.

Scrambled Eggs with Meat and Onion

BAYD BIL LAHMEH WA BUSSEL

This dish is a great way to stretch a little bit of meat. Raw green onion (scallion) is tasty to eat alongside, and of course flatbread is perfect for scooping it up.

Serves *4 as part of a maza platter or 2 as a meal*
Preparation Time: *5 minutes*
Cooking Time: *10 minutes*

2 tablespoons oil
½ lb (250 g) lean ground beef or lamb
1 onion, diced
½ teaspoon salt
⅛ teaspoon freshly ground black pepper
4 large eggs, lightly beaten
1 sprig fresh parsley leaves, chopped
(optional, for garnish)

1 Add the oil to a large nonstick skillet over moderately high heat. Add the meat and onion, and cook until the meat is browned and the onion is softened, about 5 to 7 minutes, stirring occasionally and using a wooden spoon to break up the meat. Stir in the salt and pepper.
2 Turn heat down to medium and pour in the eggs. Let the eggs cook until slightly set, about 1 minute, then gently stir upward from the bottom so the uncooked eggs are exposed to the bottom of the pan; continue stirring like this until the eggs are set, about 1 to 2 minutes more.
3 Sprinkle the parsley on top, if using.

⁖Meat Sautéed with Leeks⁖ — BELLASSIA

With three different kinds of onion in this recipe, it really is an onion lover's delight.

The leek is the star of this dish and has a pleasant, mild onion flavor without being overpowering. Traditionally, *Bellassia* is served as part of a maza platter with a variety of other dishes. Regardless of what else it's served with, flatbread is always present since it's used as a utensil to scoop up the mixture. Any leftovers will make a great omelet filling for the next day.

Serves *4 to 6 as part of a maza platter or 2 as a meal*
Preparation Time: *10 minutes*
Cooking Time: *20 minutes*

4 tablespoons oil
½ lb (250 g) lean ground beef or lamb
1 onion, diced
2 lb (1 kg) leeks, white and light green parts only, rinsed and finely diced
½ teaspoon salt
¼ teaspoon freshly ground black pepper
1 green onion (scallion), white and green parts, thinly sliced on an angle (optional, for garnish)

1 Add the oil to a large skillet over high heat. Stir in the meat and diced onion, and cook until the meat is browned and the onion is softened, about 5 to 7 minutes, stirring occasionally and using a wooden spoon to break up the meat.
2 Add the leek, salt, and pepper and cook uncovered 5 minutes, then cover the skillet, turn heat down to medium, and cook until the leeks are soft, about 5 to 7 minutes more, stirring occasionally.
3 Transfer to a serving dish. Sprinkle green onion on top, if using.

Stuffed Marrow Squash

KOUSA MAHSHI

Like any stuffed dish, Stuffed Marrow Squash can be somewhat time-consuming to make. Hollowing out the vegetables is what takes the longest, but this is best done with a group of friends and a pot of coffee on a carefree afternoon.

To reheat, bring the tomato broth to a simmer and add the marrow squash or zucchini; heat until warm, about 15 minutes.

Serves *4 to 6*
Preparation Time: *1 hour, 15 minutes*
Cooking Time: *1 hour, 25 minutes*

2 lb (2 kg) marrow squash or small zucchini, hollowed out (see Hollowing Out Vegetables to Stuff, page 12)
1 batch Lamb and Rice Stuffing (Page 28)
1 tablespoon olive oil
1 small onion, finely diced
2 cloves garlic, crushed in a mortar and pestle
Three tomatoes, peeled and diced (with their juices)
3 tablespoons tomato paste
¾ teaspoon salt
¼ teaspoon freshly ground black pepper
2 chicken or beef-flavored soft bouillon cubes
2 bay leaves
3 tablespoons minced fresh parsley leaves
1 teaspoon dried mint
1 lemon, wedged (optional, for serving
Plain yogurt (optional, for serving)

1 Prepare the Lamb and Rice Stuffing.
2 Heat the oil in a medium pot over medium heat; add the onion and cook until softened, about 5 to 7 minutes, stirring occasionally. Add the garlic and sauté 1 minute more, stirring constantly.
3 Add the tomato, tomato paste, salt, black pepper, bouillon cubes, bay leaves, fresh parsley, and enough water to fill the pot so that it is somewhere between ⅔ to ¾ of the way full (about 8 cups/1.75 liters). Heat the tomato broth over low heat until it comes to a simmer.
4 Stuff each marrow squash or zucchini shell with the Lamb & Rice Stuffing, packing the mixture down slightly so that when turned upside-down the mixture doesn't fall out. Leave about ½ to ¾ inch (1.25 to 2 cm) at the top of each because the rice will expand when cooking.
5 Add the stuffed squash to the simmering tomato broth; cover the pot and bring back up to a simmer, then cook until the rice is fully done, about 1 hour. If the squash doesn't all fit in the pot because there's too much liquid, you can just ladle out some broth. (To check if the rice is fully cooked, remove a piece of squash and cut it in half.)
6 Serve the squash alongside the tomato broth to eat as soup or to spoon on top, along with fresh lemon to squeeze on top and yogurt, if using.

❧Lamb and Barley Soup❧

SHORABET SHAREEYEH

This hearty soup is perfect for a cold day. Oregano and mint are herbs that are part of the same family and really work together well in this dish. This soup thickens after standing; to reheat any leftovers, warm it on the stovetop, adding water as necessary.

Serves *4 to 6*
Preparation Time: *10 minutes*
Cooking Time: *2 hours,*
 5 minutes (1 hour, 45 minutes
 of which is simmer time)

2 tablespoons olive oil
2 lb (1 kg) bone-in lamb
 shoulder, cut into large
 pieces and patted dry
2 onions, diced
1½ teaspoons dried oregano
½ teaspoon Nine Spice Mix
 (page 29)
¼ teaspoon salt
2 bay leaves
2 chicken or beef-flavored
 soft bouillon cubes
7 cups (1.7 liters) water
½ cup (100 g) pearl barley
1½ teaspoons dried mint
 flakes

1 Prepare Nine Spice Mix.
2 Heat the oil in a medium pot with a lid, over moderately high heat; add half the lamb and brown, allowing it to sear on all sides, about 3 to 5 minutes. Transfer the seared lamb to a bowl; sear the rest of the lamb the same way and transfer it to the bowl with the rest of the lamb.
3 Add the onion to the pot the lamb was cooked in and sauté until wilted, about 3 minutes. Add the oregano, Nine Spice Mix, salt, bay leaves, bouillon cubes, and water.
4 Bring to a boil over high heat, skimming off any foam on the surface. Turn heat down to simmer, cover the pot, and cook until the meat is tender, about 60 to 90 minutes, stirring occasionally. Add the barley and cook until tender, about 30 minutes, stirring occasionally.
5 Turn off heat and stir in the mint; serve.

❧Lamb and Navy Bean Stew❧

FAJOOM

This soup is a classic example of Syrian cooking; it's thick and rich, and heady with the aroma of spices.

Serves *6*
Preparation Time: *10 minutes*
Cooking Time: *1 hour, 20 minutes*
 (1 hour of which is simmer time)

2 tablespoons clarified butter (or
 1 tablespoon unsalted butter
 plus 1 tablespoon canola oil)
2 onions, diced
1 lb (500 g) boneless lamb
 shoulder or leg of lamb,
 trimmed of excess fat and
 cubed
2 cloves garlic, crushed in a
 mortar and pestle
2 teaspoons ground cumin
1 teaspoon Syrian Spice Mix
 (page 29)
½ teaspoon freshly ground black
 pepper
2 chicken or beef-flavored soft
 bouillon cubes
2 bay leaves
3 tablespoons tomato paste
4 cups (1 liter) water
Two 15 oz (425 g) cans navy
 beans, rinsed and drained
1 batch Rice with Toasted
 Vermicelli Noodles (page 58)
 (optional, for serving)

1 Prepare Syrian Spice Mix.
2 Heat the clarified butter in a medium pot and place over medium heat; add the onion and cook 5 minutes, stirring occasionally. Turn the heat up to high, add the lamb, and cook until browned, about 3 to 5 minutes (do not stir until it's browned on the first side). Add the garlic and cook 30 seconds, stirring constantly.
3 Stir in the cumin, Syrian Spice Mix, black pepper, bouillon cubes, bay leaves, tomato paste, and water. Bring to a boil and then cover the pot, leaving the lid slightly ajar; turn the heat down to simmer and cook until meat is tender, about 45 minutes to 1 hour, stirring occasionally. (If the stew starts to look too thick, fully cover the pot or add a splash of water.)
4 Add the beans and cook until heated through, about 3 to 5 minutes.
5 Serve alongside Rice with Toasted Vermicelli Noodles, if using.

Lamb and Yogurt Soup

SHAKREEYEH

If you didn't grow up eating this soup, it really is an acquired taste. On the other hand, if you've eaten this soup all your life you're likely to love it from a young age. (I can attest to this, as I've seen firsthand many mothers feeding this to their young ones. One mom told me, referring to her three-year-old daughter, "It's all she'll eat!") This soup is creamy but very tangy; garlic accentuates the other flavors very well. It is frequently eaten the day after Ramadan, since yogurt is good for digestion.

Serves *6*
Preparation Time: *5 minutes*
Cooking Time: *1 hour, 30 minutes (1 hour of which is simmer time)*

3 tablespoons oil, divided
1 lb (500 g) boneless lamb shoulder or leg of lamb,
    trimmed of excess fat and cubed
Water to cover the lamb (about 2½ cups/625 ml)
2 chicken or beef-flavored soft bouillon cubes
¼ teaspoon salt
2 bay leaves
2 tablespoons cornstarch, dissolved in 2 tablespoons cold water
2 lb (1 kg) plain yogurt, room temperature
3 cloves garlic, crushed
¼ teaspoon salt
1 batch Rice with Toasted Vermicelli Noodles (page 58)
    (optional, for serving)

1 Prepare Rice with Toasted Vermicelli Noodles, if using.
2 Heat 2 tablespoons of oil in a medium, heavy-bottomed pot over high heat; add the lamb and cook until browned, about 3 to 5 minutes (do not stir until it's browned on the first side).
3 Add just enough water to cover, then add the bouillon cubes, salt, and bay leaves. Bring it up to a boil, then put the lid on, turn the head down, and simmer until the meat is tender, about 45 minutes to 1 hour.
4 Mix the cornstarch and cold water in a small bowl; add the cornstarch/water slurry and the yogurt to the pot with the meat. Bring to a simmer over medium-low heat while stirring constantly in one direction with a wooden spoon; simmer 2 minutes, continuing to stir constantly.
5 Heat the remaining 1 tablespoon oil in a small pan over low heat; add the garlic, salt, and cook until fragrant and light golden, about 2 to 3 minutes, stirring constantly.
6 Add the garlic to the soup and serve with Rice with Toasted Vermicelli Noodles (Roz bil Shariya), if using.

Cauliflower Meat Sauce

M'NEZALIT ZAHARA

This dish sounds a little unusual, but it tastes surprisingly fantastic. The pomegranate molasses gives it a wonderfully complex sweet/tart flavor. Serve it spooned over Rice with Toasted Vermicelli Noodles (Roz bil Shariya) (page 58) to make it a full meal.

Serves *4 to 6*
Preparation Time: *15 minutes*
Cooking Time: *1 hour*

4 tablespoons olive oil, divided

1 large onion, diced

1 lb (500 g) boneless lamb, trimmed of excess fat and cubed

4 cloves garlic, crushed in a mortar and pestle

3 tomatoes, diced

2 tablespoons tomato paste

2 tablespoons pomegranate molasses

1 cup (250 ml) water

1 chicken or beef-flavored soft bouillon cube

¾ teaspoon salt, divided

¼ teaspoon freshly ground black pepper or 1 teaspoon Meat Spice Mix (page 29)

1 large head cauliflower, cut into florets

½ bunch coriander leaves (cilantro), minced

1 batch Rice with Toasted Vermicelli Noodles (page 58) (for serving)

1 Prepare Rice with Toasted Vermicelli Noodles.
2 Heat 2 tablespoons oil in a medium lidded saucepan over high heat; add the onion and cook 5 minutes, stirring occasionally. Turn the heat up to high, add the lamb and cook until browned, about 3 minutes. Add the garlic, tomatoes, tomato paste, and pomegranate molasses, and cook 2 minutes, stirring constantly. Add the water, bouillon cube, ½ teaspoon of salt, and black pepper. Bring it to a boil; turn the heat down to simmer, cover the saucepan, and cook until the meat is tender, about 30 to 40 minutes, stirring occasionally.
3 Preheat oven to 400°F (200°C); line a large baking sheet with parchment paper or a silpat liner. Toss the cauliflower with the remaining 2 tablespoons oil and the remaining ¼ teaspoon salt in a large bowl. Spread the cauliflower out on the prepared baking sheet and roast until golden brown in spots, about 40 minutes, stirring once halfway through.
4 When the meat is tender, add the roasted cauliflower and cilantro to the meat sauce and cook (uncovered) until the cauliflower is warmed, about 3 to 5 minutes.
5 Serve alongside Rice with Toasted Vermicelli Noodles.

Lamb or Beef Kebabs KEBAB WA KUFTA

Kebab is meat that is flavored with onion, parsley, and spices. If this mixture is cooked in a tray (instead of in a frying pan or on a grill), it's referred to as *kufta*, although the meat mixture used is the same; prepared this way, it is usually thought of as meatloaf or meatballs. Simple as it sounds, there are an endless number of different variations on this one meat mixture. My father-in-law's favorite version of this dish is the Baked with Potato and Tomato version and I learned this variant from him. Other tasty variations include a tangy tahini or yogurt-based sauce to top *kufta* that is either spread in a tray or shaped into round or oblong meatballs and then baked. In general, if you're making kebab use semi-lean meat and if you're making *kufta*, use lean.

Pan Fried Kebabs

Each variation serves *3 to 4*

Skewered Grilled Kebabs

Preparation Time: *15 minutes*
Cooking Time: *10 minutes*

1 lb (500 g) semi-lean or lean ground lamb or beef
1 small onion, grated
¼ bunch fresh parsley leaves, minced
1 teaspoon salt
1 teaspoon Seven Spice Mix (page 29)
⅛ teaspoon fresh ground black pepper

1 Use your hands to combine all ingredients in a large bowl.
2 Fill a small bowl with water for wetting your hands in between shaping the kebabs. Wet your hands and roll a small handful of the meat mixture into a ball (about the size of an egg), then slide it onto a metal skewer. Flatten the ball so the meat spreads out on the skewer, and repeat this process until all the meat is skewered.
3 Grill until fully cooked, about 8 to 10 minutes, flipping once halfway through.

VARIATION 1
Pan Fried Kebabs

Preparation Time: *10 minutes*
Cooking Time: *10 minutes*

1 batch Kebab Meat Mixture
1 tablespoon olive oil

1 Shape the meat into 8 equal patties.
2 Heat the oil in a large nonstick skillet over medium to moderately-high heat.
3 Add the patties and cook until browned outside and cooked through, about 8 to 10 minutes, flipping once.
4 Serve immediately, with Cucumber Yogurt Salad (Leban bil Khiear) (page 43), Middle Eastern Salad (Salata) (page 47), and/or Mixed White & Yellow Rice (page 61), if desired.

VARIATION 2
Baked Kebabs with Potato and Tomato KUFTA BIL SAYNIEH

Preparation Time: *15 minutes*
Cooking Time: *45 minutes*

1 batch Kebab Meat Mixture
3-4 potatoes, peeled and sliced
3-4 tomatoes, sliced
¾ teaspoon salt
¼ teaspoon freshly ground black pepper
1 tablespoon olive oil
1 tablespoon fresh lemon juice
2 tablespoons minced fresh parsley leaves (optional, for garnish)

1 Preheat oven to 400°F (200°C). Get out a 9 to 10-inch (23 to 25 cm) round baking pan (or a 9-inch/23 cm square baking pan).
2 Put the potato slices into a medium saucepan and add enough cold water to cover them by about 1 inch (2.5 cm). Bring to a boil over high heat, then turn the heat down slightly and simmer until fork-tender, about 5 to 7 minutes; drain.
3 Press the meat evenly into the bottom of the pan. Arrange the potato in an even layer on top of the meat (they should all fit with minimal overlapping), then sprinkle on ½ teaspoon salt and ⅛ teaspoon black pepper. Arrange the tomato in an even layer on top of the potato, then sprinkle on the remaining ¼ teaspoon salt and ⅛ teaspoon black pepper. Drizzle the olive oil and lemon juice on top.
4 Cover the dish bake until the meat is fully cooked, about 30 minutes, uncovering the dish about halfway through cooking so some of the liquid can evaporate. Once cooked, if you want to brown the top in spots, you can place it briefly under the broiler.
5 Cool slightly before cutting and serving; sprinkle parsley on top, if using.

Meatballs with Potato in Tomato Sauce · KEBAB HINDI

This is another variation of Lamb or Beef Kebab (page 112). It's one of my mother-in-law's specialties and it always feels like a special treat when she makes it. Funnily enough, the name literally means "Indian Kebab," although you'd be hard pressed to find anything Indian about it, or to find someone who can explain where the name comes from.

Serves *4 to 6*
Preparation Time: *25 minutes*
Cooking Time: *1 hour, 5 minutes (45 minutes of which is bake time)*

1 batch uncooked Lamb or Beef Kebab
   (opposite page)
3 tablespoons clarified butter
   (or 1½ tablespoons canola oil and
   1½ tablespoons butter)
3-4 onions, chopped
3-4 tomatoes, chopped
1 teaspoon salt
½ teaspoon Syrian Spice Mix (page 29)
⅛ teaspoon freshly ground
   black pepper
4 tablespoons tomato paste
2 cups (500 ml) water
3-4 potatoes, peeled and cut into
   wedges or cubes
1 batch Rice with Toasted Vermicelli
   Noodles (optional) (page 58)

1 Prepare Lamb or Beef Kebab, Syrian Rice Mix, and Rice with Toasted Vermicelli Noodles.
2 Fill a small bowl with water and keep it next to you so you can wet your hands while shaping the meat. Grab a small handful of the meat mixture (about 2 tablespoons) and shape it into an oblong finger-shaped piece about 2 inches (5 cm) long; repeat this process with the rest of the meat.
3 Heat the clarified butter in a large skillet over moderately-high heat; add the meatballs in a single layer and cook until browned, about 2 to 3 minutes per side, flipping once. Transfer to a plate and set aside. Preheat the oven to 350°F (175°C).
4 Add the onion to the skillet the meat was cooked in, and cook over medium heat until starting to soften, about 5 to 7 minutes, stirring occasionally. Stir in the tomato, salt, Syrian Spice Mix, and black pepper; cook 5 minutes. Add the tomato paste and water, turn heat up to high, and bring up to a boil; cook 5 minutes.
5 Transfer the tomato sauce, meatballs, and potato to a medium-sized casserole dish; cover the dish and bake until the meat is fully cooked and the potato is tender, about 45 minutes.
6 Serve with Rice with Toasted Vermicelli Noodles, if using.

Upside Down Rice Casserole   MAQLUBA

Serves 6-8

Preparation Time: *1 hour, 30 minutes*
Cooking Time: *2 hours, 20 minutes*
  *(1 hour of which is simmer time for
  the meat)*

1 lb (500 g) eggplant
1½ teaspoons salt, divided
Oil, for shallow frying
1 head cauliflower, cut into florets
3-4 potatoes, peeled and sliced
½ cup (125 ml) plus 1 tablespoon olive
  oil, divided
1 onion, diced
1 lb (500 g) boneless lamb, trimmed of
  excess fat and cubed
1½ teaspoons Nine Spice Mix (page 29),
  divided
½ teaspoon freshly ground black
  pepper, divided
¼ teaspoon ground cinnamon
2 chicken or beef-flavored soft bouillon
  cubes
4 cups (1 liter) water
1 teaspoon ground cumin
½ teaspoon ground coriander
½ teaspoon ground turmeric
2 cups (425 g) uncooked basmati rice
4 tablespoons blanched almonds or
  pine nuts
Cucumber Yogurt Salad (page 43) or
  plain yogurt (optional, for serving)

After making *Maqluba* one day, my mother-in-law told me that Middle Eastern women spend way too much time in the kitchen. I laughed, because I had just seen how much work went into this one dish! The good thing about *Maqluba* is that even though it's time consuming to make, it isn't difficult; and better still, it can be broken down into steps and portions of it can be made up to a couple days in advance.

When I make *Maqluba*, I cook the cauliflower and potato two days in advance; the day before, I make the eggplant, meat, and the Cucumber Yogurt Salad (page 43) that is served with the casserole. That way, when it comes time to actually make the dish I'm not so overwhelmed.

This is a traditional Palestinian dish that's enjoyed throughout the Levant. Of course there are as many different variations of this dish as there are families who make it. Some include tomatoes, green peppers, or thick-sliced rings of onion; others leave out potato or cauliflower. Some make it with chicken or beef instead of lamb.

Toasted nuts on top aren't essential to this dish the way they are to a few other pilafs, but they are a tasty addition. In the Middle East, nuts are generally a relatively expensive item, so adding them to any dish is thought of as a nice way to honor your guests.

1 Prepare Nine Spice Mix and Cucumber Yogurt Salad.
2 Fully or partially peel the eggplant if desired. (To partially peel it, peel one strip off down the length of the vegetable, then leave the strip next to it on and peel the next strip off, and so on). Slice into ½-inch (1.25-cm) thick slices crosswise.
3 Sprinkle 1 teaspoon salt on both sides of each slice of eggplant and transfer to a colander; put the colander in the sink and let it sit for 30 minutes (while the eggplant drains, prepare the cauliflower and potato). Rinse the eggplant under running water, then gently wring out any excess water and pat dry.
4 Coat the bottom of a large skillet over moderately high heat with oil. Fry the eggplant in batches (so the pan isn't overcrowded) until golden brown, about 2 to 4 minutes per side. (You can add more oil to the pan if necessary.) Transfer the cooked eggplant to a paper towel-lined plate to drain any excess oil.
5 Preheat oven to 400°F (200°C); line 2 large baking sheets with parchment paper or silpat liners.
6 Toss the cauliflower florets with 2 tablespoons of olive oil and ⅛ teaspoon salt; transfer to one of the prepared baking sheets. Toss the potato slices with 2 tablespoons of olive oil and ⅛ teaspoon salt; transfer to the other prepared baking sheet. Roast the veggies until they're tender and golden brown in places (about 40 minutes for the cauliflower and 30 minutes for the potato), flipping halfway through cooking.
7 Heat 2 tablespoons olive oil in a medium pot over medium heat; add the onion and cook 5 minutes, stirring occasionally. Turn the heat to high, add the lamb, and cook until browned, about 3 to 5 minutes (do not stir until it's browned on the first side).
8 Stir in 1 teaspoon of the Nine Spice Mix, ¼ teaspoon of the black pepper, cinnamon, bouillon cubes, and water. Bring to a boil and then cover the pot; turn the heat down to simmer and cook until the meat is tender, about 45 minutes to 1 hour, stirring occasionally. Use a slotted spoon to transfer the meat to a bowl; set the meat aside and reserve the liquid.

9 Soak the rice in tepid water for 15 minutes; drain. Stir together the rice, remaining ¼ teaspoon salt, remaining ½ teaspoon Nine Spice Mix, remaining ¼ teaspoon black pepper, cumin, coriander, and turmeric.

10 To layer the casserole, drizzle 1 tablespoon of olive oil on the bottom of a medium, thick-bottomed lidded saucepan. Sprinkle 2 tablespoons of rice across the bottom of the saucepan, arrange the meat on top, arrange the cauliflower on top of the meat, arrange the eggplant on top of the cauliflower, and then arrange the potato on top of the cauliflower; press the layers down gently with your hands (spread each layer as evenly as possible). Add the rest of the rice on top.

11 Bring the reserved liquid that the meat was cooked in to a boil (you can strain out the onions first if you want, but it isn't necessary) and put half a kettle of water on to boil in case you need it. Add the meat liquid so that the rice is just covered with liquid, about 4 cups (1 liter); if the meat liquid isn't enough, use boiling water.

12 Bring the casserole to a boil over moderately-high heat, then cover the pot, turn the heat down to very low, and simmer until the rice is tender, about 12 to 15 minutes, adding a splash of water if necessary.

13 Heat the remaining 2 tablespoons of olive oil in a small skillet over medium heat. Add the nuts and cook until golden brown, about 1 to 2 minutes, stirring constantly. Transfer to a small bowl and set aside.

14 Once cooked, let the rice sit with the lid on for 15 minutes, then remove the lid and place a large platter on top of the pot. Carefully invert the pot and let it sit like this for 2 minutes, then tap the bottom of the pot and gently remove it.

15 Sprinkle the nuts on top and serve with Cucumber Yogurt Salad or plain yogurt.

Date Filled Cookies
(page 118)

CHAPTER EIGHT

Desserts

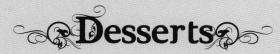

Sweets are beloved by all in the Middle East. Whether it s a tin of cookies stashed in the cupboard or a row of delicately flavored puddings lined up in the refrigerator, they are deliciously alluring and are calling out to be eaten. Some form of sweet is always on hand in Middle Eastern households. They are treats given to guests who arrive expectedly or unexpectedly, to neighbors who come to visit and chat with the woman of the house while the men are away working, and to children coming home from a day at school. They can also be found adorning an afternoon tray of coffee or an after dinner tray of tea, and even on the breakfast table, like Apple Preserves (Murabba Toofah) (page 126), Apricot Jam (Murabba Mishmish) (page 125), Sesame Fudge (Halawa) (page 119), and Toasted Semolina Pudding with Cinnamon (Mamounieh) (page 130). Some sweets are used for special celebrations, like Date Filled Cookies (Ma'amoul) (page 118) and others are used to line the pockets of the young and old alike, like Sesame Seed Brittle (Simsemieh) (page 126).

Date Filled Cookies MA'AMOUL

Ma'amoul means "stuffed" and these cookies can be stuffed with a number of different fillings. Date filling is traditional for celebrating *Eid al Fitr* (the Festival of Fast-Breaking at the end of Ramadan) and *Eid al Adha* (the Festival of Sacrifice), but walnuts (flavored either with orange blossom syrup or cinnamon) and pistachios (flavored with rose water and orange blossom water) are also common. For the walnut or pistachio filling, moisten the nuts slightly with a bit of Scented Sugar Syrup (Qater) (page 28); cinnamon can be added to the walnut filling, but if you wish to do so, omit the orange blossom water and the rose water from the sugar syrup. A different shaped mold is used for each filling, see Cookie Molds on page 16. There are two different types of dough—one is shortbread-like and doesn't contain semolina; the other contains semolina and has a coarser texture. This is the shortbread variety, which is my favorite.

Below I give directions for how to shape these cookies with a *Ma'amoul* mold, but they can also be shaped by hand. To do so, grab a small handful of dough (about 1½ tablespoons) and roll it into an egg shape. Gently insert your finger into one end (don't go through to the other side), rotating the dough as you do so; you will end up with a little well. Fill this well with about 1 teaspoon of filling and pinch the end to seal. Use your hands to gently shape it into a circle, and then slightly flatten the circle into a disc. Use a fork to make a decorative crosshatch pattern on the top.

If you have extra date filling, wrap it well and freeze for up to 6 months. When you're ready to use it, let it thaw in the fridge overnight, then knead a little bit of canola oil into it until smooth.

Yields *about 4 dozen cookies*
Preparation Time: *1 hour, 30 minutes*
Cooking Time: *35 minutes*

Date Filling
¾ lb (350 g) pitted dates, coarsely chopped
2 tablespoons oil
1½ teaspoons Cake Spice Mix (page 29)

Dough
1 cup (225 g) sugar
¾ cup (180 ml) water
¼ cup (65 ml) oil
¾ cup (175 g) clarified butter
4 cups (500 g) all-purpose flour, plus up to 4 tablespoons more for kneading
½ teaspoon instant yeast

Other
¼ cup (30 g) powdered sugar (optional, for dusting on top)

1 Prepare Cake Spice Mix.
2 To make the Date filling, grind the dates and oil in a stand mixer fitted with a food grinding attachment (fine grind) or in a heavy-duty food processor. If using a stand mixer, alternate between adding the dates and oil. If you're using a food processor, before you add any dates, rub oil on the blade and inside of the bowl. Once processed, oil your hands and knead the Cake Spice Mix into the dates.
3 To make the dough, combine the sugar and water in a small saucepan over medium heat; bring to a full, rolling boil (occasionally giving the pan a swirl), boil 1 minute, and then turn off the heat. Let it cool 5 to 10 minutes.
4 Combine oil and clarified butter in a separate small saucepan and cook over medium heat until the butter is just melted, about 2 minutes; cool slightly.
5 Put the flour in a large bowl and whisk in the yeast. Use a wooden spoon to gradually incorporate the oil mixture, then gradually incorporate the sugar syrup. Knead the dough until it comes together nicely, adding up to 4 tablespoons more flour as needed (when done, the dough will be soft and should look smooth, shiny, and slightly oily). Cover the dough, put it in the freezer to stiffen slightly, about 5 to 10 minutes, and then knead it again for a couple minutes.
6 Preheat oven to 350°F (175°C); line 2 large baking sheets with parchment paper or silpat liners.
7 To shape the cookies with a *Ma'amoul* mold, measure 1 slightly scant tablespoon of dough and roll it into a ball; slightly flatten it with your hands, then press it into the bottom and up the sides of the mold. Measure 1 teaspoon of the date mixture and roll it into a ball; slightly flatten it and gently press it into the dough in the mold. Measure 1 slightly scant teaspoon of dough, roll it into a ball, slightly flatten it, then put it on top of the date mixture in the mold; use your fingers to press the dough on the top into the dough on the sides. To remove the cookie from the mold, hold the mold by the handle and tap the flat rim on a secure surface; the cookie will drop right out.
8 Arrange the cookies on the baking sheets about ½ to 1 inch (1.25 to 2.5 cm) apart (if you use 2 half-sheet pans, the cookies should all fit on 2 pans; otherwise, you will need to cook them in 2 batches); bake until light golden brown on the bottom, about 20 to 25 minutes, rotating the trays once.
9 Cool completely, and then dust with the powdered sugar. To store the cookies, package them layered between parchment paper in an airtight container.

How to Make the Date Filled Cookies

STEP 1: Measure 1 slightly scant tablespoon of dough and roll it into a ball; slightly flatten it with your hands, then press it into the bottom and up the sides of the mold.

STEP 2: Measure 1 teaspoon of the date mixture and roll it into a ball; slightly flatten it and gently press it into the dough in the mold.

STEP 3: Measure 1 slightly scant teaspoon of dough, roll it into a ball, slightly flatten it, then put it on top of the date mixture in the mold; use your fingers to press the dough on the top into the dough on the sides.

STEP 4: To remove the cookie from the mold, hold the mold by the handle and tap the flat rim on a secure surface; the cookie will drop right out.

Sesame Fudge

HALAWA

Tahini makes very unique fudge that is deliciously sweet and nutty, with just a hint of bitterness. This fudge is frequently eaten with breakfast, spread on flatbread with a little butter.

Yields *1 loaf pan of fudge*
Preparation Time: *15 minutes, plus 24 hours for the fudge to set*
Cooking Time: *10 minutes*

2 teaspoons butter
1½ cups (350 g) tahini
1½ cups (350 g) sugar
¾ cup (185 ml) water
1 teaspoon rose water, orange blossom water, or pure vanilla extract (optional)
½ cup (60 g) shelled pistachios

1 Grease a loaf pan with the butter and set aside. Pour the tahini into a large bowl and beat with a handheld electric mixer until smooth; set aside.
2 Add the sugar and water to a medium, thick-bottomed saucepan, over medium heat; cook until it reaches the softball stage on a candy thermometer (240°F/115°C), stirring occasionally. Stir in the rose water or other flavoring, if using. Cool 2 minutes.
3 Using an electric mixer, gradually beat the sugar syrup into the tahini. Once all the syrup is beat in, continue beating it for 1 minute. Stir in the pistachios with a wooden spoon, and knead the mixture a couple times with your hands.
4 Press the mixture into the prepared loaf pan; cool to room temperature, then cover the pan with plastic wrap and refrigerate 24 hours before slicing and serving.

Layered Apricot and Milk Pudding

MUHALLIBIET QAMAR AL DEEN

Sweet/tart apricot pudding and creamy milk pudding are layered in this pretty dessert, which is a great way to use Apricot Leather (page 18).

Serves *4 to 6*
Preparation Time: *10 minutes, plus 2 to 12 hours to for the apricot leather to soak, and time for the pudding to chill*
Cooking Time: *15*

Rose & Orange Blossom-Scented Milk Pudding
2 cups (500 ml) milk, divided
4 tablespoons cornstarch
4 tablespoons sugar
½ teaspoon rose water
½ teaspoon orange blossom water

Apricot Pudding
2 cups (500 ml) hot water
4 tablespoons sugar
½ lb (250 g) apricot leather or dried apricots, torn or chopped into pieces
4 tablespoons cornstarch dissolved in 4 tablespoons cold water
1 teaspoon orange blossom water

Garnish
2 tablespoons shelled pistachios, chopped

NOTE: At least 4½ hours before you want to serve the pudding, soak the apricot leather and make the milk pudding so the bottom layer has time to set.

1 To soak the apricot leather: Combine the water and sugar in a large measuring cup with a pour spout, stirring until the sugar is completely dissolved. Put the pieces of apricot leather in a large bowl and pour the water/sugar mixture on top. Cover, and let sit 2 to 12 hours.

2 To make the milk pudding: Whisk together ½ cup (125 ml) milk with the cornstarch in a small bowl and set aside. Combine the sugar and remaining 1½ cups (375 ml) milk in a medium-sized, heavy-bottomed saucepan over medium heat; cook until it comes to a boil, stirring occasionally. Whisk the cornstarch mixture into the boiling milk and cook 1 minute, whisking constantly. Turn off the heat and stir in the rose water and orange blossom water. Pour into 4 to 6 individual serving cups, filling each cup halfway full; cool to room temperature and then refrigerate 2 to 12 hours. *At least 2½ hours before you want to serve the pudding, make the apricot pudding layer from the soaked apricot leather.*

3 Purée the apricot leather and water in a blender or food processor; strain through a fine mesh sieve.

4 Heat the apricot purée in a medium-sized, heavy-bottomed saucepan over medium heat until it comes to a boil, stirring occasionally. Whisk the cornstarch/water mixture into the boiling apricot puree and cook 2 minutes, whisking constantly. Turn off heat and stir in the orange blossom water.

5 Pour the apricot pudding on top of the milk pudding; cool to room temperature and then refrigerate to chill, about 2 hours.

Lebanese Nights

LAYALI LUBNAN

Puddings are a huge part of Middle Eastern sweets. This isn't so much because they're easier or faster to prepare than other sweets, but because they're the perfect treat to keep in your fridge for when a neighbor, family member, or friend pops by unannounced.

This pudding is one of my absolute favorites. The pudding itself is rich and velvety, and it's topped with a layer of whipped cream, a drizzle of Scented Sugar Syrup (page 28), and a sprinkle of pistachios and coconut. Instead of whipped cream, *Ishta* is traditionally used (see Clotted Cream, page 25 for more information on *Ishta*); however, *Ishta* is much thicker and heavier, and I prefer the lightness of whipped cream.

The name of this pudding is so much fun; to me, it conjures up images of nighttime merriment: eating, drinking, and storytelling. I always end up picturing Shahrazad and the mystic stories from *1001 Nights and a Night*.

For a completely different flavor, omit the mastic, orange blossom water, and rose water, and use 1½ teaspoons of pure vanilla extract (or ½ a pod of vanilla) instead.

Serves *6*
Preparation Time: *10 minutes, plus time for the pudding to chill*
Cooking Time: *10 minutes*

½ batch Scented Sugar Syrup (page 28), cooled to room
 temperature
2 tablespoons clarified butter (or 1 tablespoon unsalted
 butter plus 1 tablespoon canola oil)
½ cup (80 g) fine semolina
4 cups (1 liter) milk
¼ teaspoon mastic (gum Arabic), ground in a mortar and
 pestle (optional)
¾ teaspoon orange blossom water
¾ teaspoon rose water
1 cup (250 ml) heavy cream
3 tablespoons shelled pistachios, chopped
3 tablespoons unsweetened, desiccated coconut

1 Prepare Scented Sugar Syrup.
2 Melt the clarified butter in a medium, thick-bottomed saucepan over medium heat; stir in the semolina and cook 2 minutes. Whisk in the milk and mastic, if using, and bring up to a boil, whisking frequently. Turn heat down to medium-low and cook until thickened, about 3 to 5 minutes, whisking constantly.
3 Turn off the heat and stir in the orange blossom water and rose water. Pour into 6 individual serving cups (or 1 large serving bowl), cool to room temperature, then refrigerate to chill.
4 Right before serving, whip the heavy cream to soft peaks and spoon it onto the semolina pudding. Drizzle on the sugar syrup to taste and sprinkle the pistachio and coconut on top.

Sweet Cheese Pastry   KNAFEH BIL JIBEN

In the Middle East, *Knafeh* is served for just about any important family gathering you can imagine. On my honeymoon I remember my husband waking up hungry one morning and going to the fridge to look for something to eat; he found half a tray of *Knafeh* leftover from our wedding reception and immediately started eating it. "I can't help it…it's just so good!" he explained when I found him, standing in front of the fridge, a mouth full of *Knafeh*, and more in his hand. At that point, I had never had *Knafeh* so I had no idea what he meant. One night a couple days later, both Mike and I had a sweet tooth; of course being a total chocolate lover I was thinking of something *chocolaty*. Mike took me to a local bakery and ordered *Knafeh* for us, insisting that I would not be disappointed. I was skeptical at first (since there is no chocolate in *Knafeh*), but he was right…it was love at first bite.

Knafeh is originally a Palestinian dessert made with a Palestinian cheese called Nabulsi, but there are many variations with different cheese or cream fillings. In this version I use a combination of soft (farmer's or Jiben Belaadi) and semi-firm (Nabulsi, Ackawi, or fresh mozzarella) white cheeses. For the soft cheese, you can use ricotta instead of farmer's cheese, if you prefer. I give instructions below on how to remove the saltiness from Nabulsi or Ackawi.

Serves *10 to 12*
Preparation Time: *15 minutes, plus 2 to 4 hours to soak the cheese if using Nabulsi or Ackawi*
Cooking Time: *40 minutes*

1 batch Scented Sugar Syrup (page 28), cooled to room temperature
¼ lb (100 g) Nabulsi, Ackawi, or fresh mozzarella cheese
¾ lb (350 g) farmer's cheese (Jiben Beladi)
3-6 tablespoons milk
½ cup (115 g) plus 1 tablespoon clarified butter or unsalted butter, divided

1 lb (500 g) frozen shredded phyllo dough (kataifi), thawed in the fridge overnight
1 tablespoon shelled pistachios, finely chopped

1 Prepare the Scented Sugar Syrup.
2 If you're using Nabulsi or Ackawi cheese, remove the saltiness by soaking the cheese in cold water for 2 to 4 hours (or overnight), changing the water several times; pat dry. Crumble the Nabulsi or Ackawi with your fingers, or grate the mozzarella; combine it with the farmer's cheese in a medium bowl, stirring in the milk 1 tablespoon at a time so that the mixture comes together into a creamy consistency (you may not need all the milk); refrigerate until ready to use.
3 Preheat oven to 450°F (230°C) and line a large baking sheet with parchment paper or a silpat liner.
4 Melt ½ cup (125 g) butter and allow to cool slightly. Place the shredded phyllo dough in a large bowl and use your hands to separate each strand. Add the butter and rub it into each strand of dough.
5 Transfer the buttered dough to the prepared baking sheet and bake until golden and crispy, about 10 to 12 minutes, stirring every 3 minutes so the edges don't burn. Cool slightly, then use your hands to crunch up the dough so you end up with pieces about ¼-inch (6 mm) in length.
6 Preheat oven (from the lower heating elements) to 400°F (200°C) and position a rack in the lower ⅓ of the oven. Spread the remaining 1 tablespoon of butter inside a round, 9 to 10-inch (23 to 25 cm) diameter spring form baking pan.
7 Spread ½ of the dough evenly into the bottom of the pan, pressing the dough down firmly with your hands. Spread the cheese on top, leaving a border of about ¼ inch (6 mm) all the way around. Evenly spread the rest of the dough on top of the cheese, pressing firmly with your hands and then evening out the surface with a spatula.
8 Bake until the cheese is melted and the dough on the outside is golden brown and has slightly pulled away from the outside of the pan, about 20 to 30 minutes. (Give the pan a gentle shake and the pastry should move freely.) Once out of the oven, drizzle ½ cup Scented Sugar Syrup on top.
9 Cool 5 minutes, then run a knife along the outside of the pan and gently remove the spring form sides. Sprinkle the pistachio on top (in a decorative pattern, if you like).
10 Serve immediately, along with the remaining ½ cup Scented Sugar Syrup to drizzle on top.

Butter Cookies GRAYBEH

These delicate butter cookies are similar to shortbread but with a hint of floral flavor. You can use either clarified butter or unsalted butter, but clarified butter is highly recommended to achieve the best flavor and texture.

These cookies can be shaped just about any way you like; however, diamonds, balls, rings, or "S" shapes are traditional. Once shaped, each cookie is decorated with a pine nut, blanched almond, or raw pistachio.

Yields *about 3 dozen cookies*
Preparation Time: *30 minutes*
Cooking Time: *25 minutes*

1 cup (250 g) clarified butter, at room temperature
1 cup (125 g) powdered sugar
2 teaspoons rose water or orange blossom water
2½ cups (320 g) all-purpose flour
4 tablespoons blanched almonds (or pine nuts or
　raw pistachios)

1 Preheat oven to 300°F (150°C); line 2 baking sheets with parchment paper or silpat liners.
2 Beat the butter, sugar, and rose water or orange blossom water together with a handheld electric mixer until light and fluffy. Gradually stir in the flour with a wooden spoon.
3 To briefly chill the dough, cover the bowl with plastic wrap and put in the fridge or freezer just until the dough stiffens slightly (about 7 minutes in the freezer).
4 Shape the cookies (see headnote above for tips) and lightly press 1 nut into each, then place them 1 inch (2.5 cm) apart on a baking sheet. Bake until they're set and golden on the bottom, but are still white on the top, about 20 to 25 minutes.
5 Cool 5 minutes on the tray and then transfer to a wire rack to finish cooling.

For Diamonds
Chill the dough 10 minutes in the fridge. Roll it out between two pieces of parchment paper (or on a lightly floured surface) to a circle about 1 inch (2.5 cm) thick and 6½ inches (16.5 cm) in diameter. With a sharp knife, cut the dough into 1-inch (2.5 cm) diamonds; place one nut in the center of each diamond. Re-roll the dough scraps and repeat this process, or make scraps into any shape you like (balls work well).

For Balls
Scoop out 1 tablespoon of dough, roll it into a ball and gently press one nut into the center.

For Rings
Form the dough into a ball, and then roll it with your hands into a rope about 3 to 4 inches (7.5 to 10 cm) long. Bring the two ends of the rope together to form a ring, and gently press one nut into the cookie where the two ends meet.

For "S" Shapes
Form the dough into a ball, and then roll it with your hands into a rope about 2 inches (5 cm) long. Form the rope into an "S" shape and gently press one nut into the center.

❧Middle Eastern Pancakes❧ QATAYEF

These sweet treats have several variations and are often served as a special occasion dessert.

Yields *about 22 pancakes*
Preparation Time: *5 minutes, plus 1 hour for the batter to rest*
Cooking Time: *20 minutes*

2 cups (250 g) all-purpose flour
2 teaspoons sugar
½ teaspoon instant yeast
¼ teaspoon baking powder
1 cup (250 ml) lukewarm milk
1 cup (250 ml) lukewarm water
1 batch Scented Sugar Syrup (page 28) (for serving)
4 tablespoons shelled pistachios, finely chopped (for serving)

1 Prepare Scented Sugar Syrup.
2 Whisk together the flour, sugar, yeast, and baking powder in a medium bowl, then whisk in the milk and water. Cover the bowl with a towel and let it sit at room temperature until bubbly and slightly risen, about 1 hour.
3 Preheat a nonstick frying pan or griddle over moderately high heat. Scoop out the batter (without stirring it) using a 2 tablespoon measure and slightly spread out the batter with the back of a spoon; cook on one side only until it's golden brown on the bottom and the top has holes and looks dry, about 1 to 2 minutes. (Do not move the pancake while it's cooking.)
4 Transfer to a parchment paper-lined surface and cool completely before stacking. Repeat this process until all the batter is cooked.
5 To serve, drizzle with Scented Sugar Syrup and sprinkle with pistachio, or make into one of the variations.

VARIATION 1
Crispy Fried Stuffed Pancakes

In this variation, *Qatayef* are filled with either soft white unsalted cheese, Clotted Cream (Ishta) (page 25), or flavored walnuts, and then sealed shut to form a half-moon shape. It doesn't stop there though…it's then deep fried until crisp (the traditional method) or crisped a bit in a hot oven. After that it's doused with Scented Sugar Syrup (page 28) and sprinkled with pistachio. This version is by far my favorite way to eat *Qatayef*.

Other options for fillings:
3 cups (850 g) soft white unsalted cheese (such as farmer's or ricotta cheese)
3 cups (850 g) or 1½ batches Clotted Cream (page 25)
3 cups (350 g) cinnamon or orange blossom scented walnuts (see the recipe for Date-Filled Cookies on page 118 for more information these two variations on walnut fillings)

Other
Oil (for frying) or 6 tablespoons melted clarified butter (for baking)
1 batch Scented Sugar Syrup (page 28), cooled to room temperature
4 tablespoons shelled pistachios, finely chopped

1 Prepare Scented Sugar Syrup.
2 Fold 1 pancake in half and pinch together 1 end; keep pinching along the edge until it is halfway closed. Spoon in about 2 teaspoons of the filling of your choice and pinch the rest of the pancake closed. Repeat this process with the remaining pancakes.
3 The pancakes can be crisped by deep-frying or in the oven. To deep fry, fill a large, heavy-bottomed pot ⅓ of the way full with canola oil and heat over moderately high heat to 350 to 375°F (175 to 190°C); add the stuffed pancakes (working in batches) and fry until golden, about 2 to 4 minutes. For the oven method, preheat the oven to 400°F (200°C) and grease a large baking sheet with 2 tablespoons of clarified butter. Arrange the *Qatayef* in a single layer on the prepared baking sheet, brush the tops with the remaining 4 tablespoons of clarified butter, and bake until crisp, about 15 to 25 minutes.
4 While the *Qatayef* is still hot, pour on the cooled Scented Sugar Syrup. Sprinkle the pistachio on top and serve.

Background: Cheese or
Cream-Filled Pancakes
with Pistachios Foreground:
Crispy Fried Stuffed pacakes

VARIATION 2
Cheese or Cream Filled Pancakes with Pistachios

This version of *Qatayef* is the most elegant, with its dainty but sumptuous look. The pancakes are left half open, then filled with Clotted Cream (Istha) (page 25) or soft white unsalted cheese, and dipped in pistachios. A bit of Scented Sugar Syrup (Qater) (page 28) drizzled on top completes them and provides a nice glistening sheen.

1 batch of Middle Eastern Pancake Batter

Filling Suggestions
3 cups (1¾ lb/850g) soft white unsalted cheese (such as farmer's or ricotta cheese)
About 3 cups or 1½ batches Clotted Cream (page 25)

Other
½ cup (60 g) shelled pistachios, finely chopped
1 batch Scented Sugar Syrup (page 28), cooled completely

1 Fold 1 pancake in half and pinch together 1 end; keep pinching along the edge until it is halfway to ⅔ of the way closed. Pipe in about 2 to 3 tablespoons of the filling of your choice, then dip the filling in the pistachios. Transfer to a tray and repeat this process with the remaining pancakes.
2 Serve immediately, with the Scented Sugar Syrup drizzled on top.

Apricot Jam
MURABBA MISHMISH

Fresh, sweet apricots are one of summer's delights; this jam is a wonderful way to preserve them for year-round use.

Yields *about 3⅓ cups (800 ml)*
Preparation Time: *10 minutes, plus 12 hours for the fruit to macerate*
Cooking Time: *50 minutes*

2 lb (1 kg) fresh apricots, washed and dried
2¼ cups (500 g) sugar
3 tablespoons fresh lemon juice

1 Cut the apricots in half and remove the pits. If the fruit is small, leave the apricots halved; if the fruit is larger, cut each half in half.
2 Combine the apricots, sugar, and lemon juice in a large bowl; cover the bowl and let it sit 12 hours at room temperature, stirring occasionally.
3 Pour the apricots along with the liquid that has collected into a heavy-bottomed medium saucepan. Bring to a boil over high heat, then turn heat down to simmer and cook 40 minutes, stirring occasionally at first and more frequently toward the end.
4 Carefully transfer the jam to sterilized jars. Cool to room temperature, and then store in the fridge.

Apple Preserves

MURABBA TOOFAH

This recipe is really a two-for-one, since you end up with not only delicious preserved apples, but also a delicious apple-scented syrup. The syrup is about as thick as honey and can be used the same way, or as a substitute for Scented Sugar Syrup (page 28).

Yields *1 quart (1 liter) of apples in syrup, plus about 1 pint (500 ml) of extra syrup*
Preparation Time: *40 minutes, plus 12 hours for the fruit to macerate*
Cooking Time: *1 hour*

Cold water to fill a large bowl ⅔ full
6 tablespoons fresh lemon juice, divided
2 lb (1 kg) organic firm, tart apples (such as Granny Smith), washed and dried
4½ cups (1 kg) sugar
1 cup (250 ml) water

1 Fill a large bowl ⅔ full with cold water and add 3 tablespoons lemon juice; keep this next to you as you prepare the apples.
2 Peel the apples, remove the core, and then cut each into quarters, dropping them in the bowl of lemon water as you go. When you're done preparing the apples, drain them and pat dry.
3 Combine the apples and sugar in a large bowl; cover the bowl and let it sit 12 hours at room temperature, stirring occasionally.
4 Pour the apples along with the liquid that has been collected into a heavy-bottomed large saucepan. Add the 1 cup (250 ml) of water and bring to a rolling boil over medium heat.
5 Stir in the remaining 3 tablespoons lemon juice, turn the heat down slightly, and simmer (uncovered) until the apples are tender (a paring knife inserted into an apple should slide right out), about 15 to 20 minutes.
6 Carefully transfer the apples to a 1-quart (1 liter) sterilized jar and pour enough syrup in to cover; pour the extra syrup into a separate 1-pint (500 ml) sterilized jar.
7 Store the jar of apples and the jar of syrup at room temperature for up to 3 months.

Sesame Seed Brittle

SIMSEMIEH

Like Sesame Fudge (page 119), this brittle is another fantastic sweet use for sesame seeds.

Yields *about ¾ lb/350 g*
Preparation Time: *10 minutes*
Cooking Time: *25 minutes*

2 teaspoons oil, plus more to oil a spatula and a knife
1 cup (140 g) hulled or unhulled sesame seeds
1 cup (225 g) sugar
1 teaspoon orange blossom water

1 Brush oil on the bottom and sides of an 8- x 8-inch (20 x 20 cm) baking pan, and lightly brush oil on a metal spatula and a sharp knife; set aside.
2 Preheat oven to 350°F (175°C). Spread the sesame seeds on a baking sheet and roast until light golden brown, about 10 to 12 minutes, stirring once halfway through. Once they're done roasting, immediately transfer to a medium bowl.
3 Add the sugar and orange blossom water to a medium-sized thick-bottomed pot; cook over moderately high heat until sugar is melted, about 5 to 8 minutes. Don't stir until about two-thirds of the sugar is melted; from that point on, gently stir constantly with a wooden spoon or heat-safe rubber spatula.
4 Once all the sugar is melted, working quickly but carefully, stir in the sesame seeds and pour the mixture into the oiled pan; smooth the surface with the oiled spatula. Cool 2 minutes, and then use the oiled knife to score 1-to 2- inch (2.5 to 5 cm) squares, rectangles, or diamonds.
5 Cool 2 to 4 minutes more, then turn out onto a cutting board and cut along the scored lines. Cool completely and store in an airtight container at room temperature, or wrap individually.

Rose and Orange Blossom Scented Milk Pudding

MUHALLIBEH

I see a pretty white pudding like this and I immediately think of vanilla, but this pudding is actually flavored with rose and orange blossom. A common flavor pairing for many Middle Eastern sweets, rose water and orange blossom water are often used to flavor things like cakes, ice creams, puddings, and pastries.

The first time I had this pudding was at a bustling ice cream parlor called Bakdash in the middle of an old market in Damascus called Souk al Hamidiya. I've made this pudding in the style that is served there: half of the top is decorated with whole blanched almonds and the other half with coarsely chopped pistachios, and a whole maraschino cherry is placed in the center.

Serves *4 to 6*
Preparation Time: *5 minutes, plus time for the pudding to chill*
Cooking Time: *10 minutes*

4 cups (1 liter) milk, divided
⅓ cup (50 g) cornstarch
6 tablespoons sugar
¾ teaspoon rose water
¾ teaspoon orange blossom water
4 tablespoons shelled pistachios, coarsely chopped
4 tablespoons blanched almonds halves
4 to 6 maraschino cherries

1 Whisk together ½ cup (125 ml) milk with the cornstarch in a small bowl and set aside.
2 Combine the sugar and remaining milk in a medium-sized, heavy-bottomed saucepan over medium heat; cook until it comes to a boil, stirring occasionally.
3 Whisk the cornstarch mixture into the boiling milk and cook 2 minutes, stirring constantly. Turn off heat and stir in the rose water and orange blossom water.
4 Pour into 4 to 6 individual serving cups, cool to room temperature, then refrigerate to chill.
5 For each pudding, decorate the top with half pistachios and half almonds, and place a cherry in the center; serve chilled.

Pistachio Sesame Cookies

BARAZEK

Along with Butter Cookies (page 123), these cookies are a treat that can be found hiding in just about every house's pantry in Damascus. These two kinds of cookies are normally served together with Turkish Coffee (page 139), and they make the perfect treat for unexpected visitors.

Yields *about 2 dozen cookies*
Preparation Time: *35 minutes*
Cooking Time: *20 minutes*

½ cup (120 g) sugar
4½ tablespoons water, divided
1½ cups (200 g) all-purpose flour
½ teaspoon baking powder
½ cup (115 g) clarified butter or unsalted butter,
   at room temperature
1½ tablespoons honey
½ cup (70 g) sesame seeds
4 tablespoons shelled pistachios, coarsely chopped

1 Preheat oven to 350°F (175°C); line 2 baking sheets with parchment paper or silpat liners.
2 Add the sugar and 4 tablespoons water to a small, thick-bottomed saucepan, and bring to a boil over medium heat, giving the pan an occasional swirl; boil 1 minute, then turn heat off and cool 10 minutes.
3 Whisk together the flour and baking powder in a small bowl. Cream the butter in a medium bowl with a wooden spoon; alternate between stirring in a bit of the sugar syrup and a bit of the flour until everything is incorporated. Cover the bowl with plastic wrap and put in the fridge or freezer just until the dough is stiff enough to handle (about 7 minutes in the freezer).
4 Stir together the honey and remaining ½ tablespoon of water in a shallow bowl; stir in the sesame seeds. Pour the pistachios into another shallow bowl.
5 Scoop out 1 tablespoon of dough, roll it into a ball, and then flatten it slightly. Dip the bottom side of a cookie in the pistachios, then dip the top side in the sesame seed/honey mixture. Place the cookie (pistachio side-down) onto the prepared baking sheet and use the back of a spoon to spread it out to a circle about 1½ inches (3.75 cm) in diameter. Continue this process with the rest of the dough, leaving about 2 to 3 inches (5 to 7.5 cm) between each cookie when you arrange them on the baking sheets.
6 Bake the cookies until golden on the edges, about 14 to 16 minutes, rotating the trays once. Let the cookies cool completely on the trays before removing.

❧Rice Pudding❧ ROZ BIL HALEEB

The two versions of this dish that I give are very different; the first (which is thickened with cornstarch) is a light, creamy milk pudding with occasional bits of cooked rice. The second (which is thickened only with rice) has a much more velvety feel on the tongue. That being said, the second version does have a drawback: it takes quite a bit longer to make. (*Note:* The kinds of rice used are different in each version. The first recipe uses medium-grain rice and the second uses short-grain rice, which is much starchier.)

For a completely different flavor for either version, omit the rose water and orange blossom water; instead, use 1½ teaspoons of pure vanilla extract (or ½ a pod of vanilla) and/or ¾ teaspoon of ground cinnamon.

Serves *4 to 6*
Preparation Time: *5 minutes*
Cooking Time: *30 minutes*

4 cups (1 liter) milk, divided
4 tablespoons cornstarch
4 tablespoons uncooked medium-grain white rice,
   quickly rinsed
1 cup (250 ml) water
6 tablespoons sugar
¾ teaspoon rose water
¾ teaspoon orange blossom water
4 tablespoons shelled pistachios, chopped

1 Whisk together ½ cup (125 ml) of milk with the cornstarch in a small bowl; set aside.
2 Bring the rice and water to a boil in a medium-sized, heavy-bottomed saucepan over medium heat; cover the saucepan, turn the heat down to simmer, and cook 12 minutes, stirring occasionally.
3 While the rice cooks, combine the remaining milk and sugar in another medium saucepan over medium heat; cook until the sugar is dissolved and the milk starts to steam, stirring occasionally. Turn off the heat.
4 When the rice is cooked, add the warm milk, cover the saucepan, and bring to a simmer over low heat, stirring occasionally; cook 5 minutes, stirring frequently. Stir in the cornstarch/milk mixture, bring to a boil, and boil uncovered for 3 minutes, stirring constantly. Remove from the heat and stir in the rose water and orange blossom water.
5 Pour into 4 to 6 individual serving cups, cool to room temperature, then refrigerate to chill.
6 Serve chilled, garnished with the pistachios.

VARIATION
Rice Pudding without Cornstarch

Preparation Time: *5 minutes*
Cooking Time: *1 hour, 15 minutes*

4 cups (1 liter) milk
2 cups (500 ml) water
6 tablespoons sugar
6 tablespoons uncooked short-grain white rice, quickly rinsed
¾ teaspoon rose water
¾ teaspoon orange blossom water
4 tablespoons shelled pistachios, chopped

1 Bring the milk, water, and sugar up to a boil in a medium-sized, heavy-bottomed saucepan over medium heat, stirring frequently; stir in the rice.
2 Turn heat down to simmer and cook (uncovered) until the rice is tender and the liquid is thickened, about 50 to 60 minutes, stirring occasionally at first but more frequently as it cooks, and then stirring constantly for the last 5 or 10 minutes. Remove from heat and stir in the rose water and orange blossom water.
3 Pour into 4 to 6 individual serving cups, cool to room temperature, then refrigerate to chill.
4 Serve chilled, garnished with the pistachios.

Coconut Semolina Cake

HARISSA

This lovely rustic cake gets its unique texture from semolina. Coconut adds additional texture and Scented Sugar Syrup (Qater) (page 28) sweetens it and keeps it moist. This cake is referred to as *Basbousa* or *Namoura*, depending on location.

Serves *10 to 12*
Preparation Time: *20 minutes*
Cooking Time: *35 minutes, plus 2 hours to let the cake absorb the syrup after cooking*

2 batches Scented Sugar Syrup (page 28)
1 tablespoon tahini, to grease the baking pan
2 cups (305 g) fine semolina flour
2 teaspoons baking powder
½ cup (115 g) sugar
½ cup (115 g) unsalted butter, room temperature
1½ cups (375 ml) milk
1 cup (75 g) desiccated, unsweetened coconut
3 tablespoons blanched almonds

1 Prepare the Scented Sugar Syrup.
2 Preheat oven to 375°F (190°C); brush the tahini on the inside of a 10-inch (25 cm) round baking pan.
3 Whisk together the semolina, baking powder, and sugar in a large bowl. Stir in the butter and then the milk until combined.
4 Transfer the batter to the prepared pan and spread it out evenly; let it sit for 10 minutes.
5 Score the batter into 1-inch (2.5 cm) square or diamond shapes with a sharp knife, periodically dipping the knife in hot water and drying it off before continuing to score the batter; place 1 almond in the center of each diamond.
6 Bake until the sides and top are golden brown, about 30 minutes. (If the sides are brown but the top isn't, you can broil the cake for a couple minutes to brown the top.)
7 Once out of the oven, cut the cake along the lines you scored. Slowly pour the cooled syrup onto the hot cake. Let the cake sit at room temperature 2 hours to absorb the syrup before serving.

Toasted Semolina Pudding with Cinnamon MAMOUNIEH

Unlike most puddings that are usually served as dessert, this pudding is more commonly eaten for breakfast. A de-salted cheese that melts nicely is a common addition or accompaniment and adds flavor, texture, and protein. (See Middle Eastern Cheese on page 21.)

Serves *4*
Preparation Time: *2 minutes*
Cooking Time: *15 minutes*

3 cups (750 ml) water
½ cup (120 g) sugar
4 tablespoons clarified butter (or 2 tablespoons unsalted butter and 2 tablespoons canola oil)
½ cup (80 g) semolina flour
¼ teaspoon cinnamon, plus more to sprinkle on top
¾ teaspoon rose water
¾ teaspoon orange blossom water

1 Add the water and sugar to a medium, thick-bottomed saucepan, and bring to a simmer over medium heat, giving the pan an occasional swirl. Once simmering, turn off heat and stir to fully dissolve sugar.
2 Melt the clarified butter in a medium, thick-bottomed saucepan over medium-low heat; stir in the semolina and cook until it's a light golden color and nutty smelling, about 3 to 5 minutes.
3 Add the sugar water, turn the heat up to medium, and bring up to a boil; turn the heat down to simmer and cook until thickened to your desired consistency, about 3 to 5 minutes, whisking constantly.
4 Turn off the heat and stir in the cinnamon, rose water, and orange blossom water. Pour into 4 individual serving cups, cool to room temperature and then refrigerate to chill.
5 Before serving, sprinkle a little more cinnamon on top.

Rose and Pistachio Ice Cream

AIMA'A

This ice cream basically tastes like Rose and Orange Blossom-Scented Milk Pudding (page 127), but in ice cream form. Like that pudding, this ice cream is famous in the Bakdash Ice Cream Parlor in Damascus's Souk al Hamidiya. There you can see the ice cream being first beaten and then stretched; it's the mastic that gives it its chewy, taffy-like quality.

Serves *16*
Preparation Time: *5 minutes, plus time for the ice cream to chill and process in an ice cream maker*
Cooking Time: *35 minutes*

2 tablespoons *sahlab* powder mix (or 2 tablespoons cornstarch plus ½ teaspoon orange blossom water)
8 cups (1.75 liters) plus 2 tablespoons whole milk, divided
2 cups (450 g) sugar
⅓ teaspoon gum mastic (gum Arabic), ground in a mortar and pestle
1½ teaspoons rose water
½ cup (55 g) finely chopped pistachios (for serving)

1 Dissolve the *sahlab* in 2 tablespoons of milk in a small bowl. Combine the dissolved *sahlab* with the remaining 8 cups (1.75 liters) of milk, sugar, and mastic in a thick-bottomed medium-large saucepan over medium heat.
2 Bring up to a boil, stirring frequently; boil for 2 minutes, stirring constantly. Turn off the heat and stir in the rose water, then strain through a fine mesh sieve.
3 Cool to room temperature, then refrigerate until well chilled (about 2 hours).
4 Transfer the chilled mixture to an ice cream machine and process according to the manufacturer's directions.
5 Once processed, put the ice cream in a freezer-safe bowl and transfer to the freezer to set (about 2 to 4 hours). While the ice cream is setting in the freezer, take it out and give it a stir every so often.
6 When you're ready to serve the ice cream, let it sit at room temperature until slightly softened, about 5 to 10 minutes. Scoop out the amount of ice cream you're serving into a large bowl, and stir it with a large metal spoon (like you would stir a cake batter) until it's smooth and creamy, about 3 to 5 minutes. Transfer to individual serving bowls and sprinkle ½ tablespoon of chopped pistachios on top of each serving.

Fresh Limeade
(page 136)

CHAPTER NINE

Drinks

A great amount of detail goes into every aspect of Middle Eastern cuisine; even drinks get the attention they deserve. Beverages in Middle Eastern culture have signifcance; when a guest arrives they are immediately offered a beverage to show your hospitality toward them (and for the guest, it's customary to accept, lest your host think you're rejecting his hospitality!). Also, during the holy month of Ramadan, when you can t eat or drink all day, special care is taken to make a delicious drink to be enjoyed at sunset when you can break your fast, the Apricot Drink (Qamar al Deen) on page 138, is a Ramadan favorite. Because of the hot climate, many drinks are served iced, like the Fresh Limeade (Limonada) (page 136) and Grape Syrup Drink with Sultanas and Pine Nuts (Jallab) on page 134), but a great variety of teas and coffees are also enjoyed, such as Sage Tea (Shai Maramieh) on page 138, Turkish Coffee (Qaweh Turkiyeh) on page 139, and White Coffee (Qahweh Bayda) on page 139.

Grape Syrup Drink with Sultanas and Pine Nuts

JALLAB

Jallab is a kind of syrup flavored mainly with grape molasses, dates, and rose water; the really interesting thing is that it's smoked with incense, which lends a smoky, spicy flavor to the drink. Instead of attempting to smoke the syrup, I add a few spices and infuse it with a smoky tea, Lapsang Souchong (if you can't find this, one or two drops of Liquid Hickory Smoke Flavor will work…but use it sparingly, since it's very potent!).

Once the syrup is made, it's diluted with water and topped with crushed ice, sultanas, and pine nuts for a refreshing treat.

Yields *6 servings*
Preparation Time: *5 minutes*
Cooking Time: *20 minutes*

¼ cup (55 g) chopped pitted dates
½ cup (125 ml) grape molasses
¾ cup (185 ml) water
1 teaspoon looseleaf Lapsang Souchong tea
One (2 in/5 cm) cinnamon stick
2 pods cardamom, bruised
2 whole cloves
1 tablespoon rose water
5 cups (1.25 liters) cold water (or more to taste)
Crushed ice for 6 glasses
6 tablespoons sultanas (golden raisins)
6 tablespoons pine nuts

1 Combine the dates, grape molasses, ¾ cup (185 ml)of water, tea, cinnamon stick, cardamom and cloves in a medium saucepan over medium heat. Bring to a boil, then turn the heat down to simmer and cook until it is syrupy and reduced by about half, about 10 to 15 minutes, stirring frequently. While cooking, occasionally mash the dates against the inside of the saucepan with the back of a wooden spoon. Stir in the rose water.
2 Strain the syrup through a fine mesh sieve, pressing gently with the back of a wooden spoon to extract all the liquid; cool to room temperature. (If you're not using it right away, store the syrup in the fridge up to 2 months before diluting it with water.)
3 Mix the syrup with 5 cups of cold water, adding more water as desired. Line a mesh sieve with a coffee filter and place it inside a bowl; strain the drink, collecting the liquid in the bowl below.
4 Fill 6 glasses with crushed ice and pour in the drink; top each glass with 1 tablespoon of sultanas and 1 tablespoon of pine nuts.

Creamy Hot Sahlab Drink

SAHLAB

Sahlab is a starchy powder made from dried orchids that is used to make creamy, rich drinks or puddings. *Sahlab* can be a difficult ingredient to find outside Turkey where it is harvested, as the orchids it is derived from are becoming rare. *Sahlab* powder mix, which is typically a mixture of cornstarch, sugar, and flavorings, can usually be found in Middle Eastern grocery stores; if you can't find this mix you can substitute cornstarch with a bit of orange blossom water.

In drink form, *sahlab* is thick and comforting...the perfect way to warm up on a cold winter day. If you prefer to make it as a pudding, increase the *sahlab* powder mix to ⅓ cup (50 grams) and keep all other amounts the same; eat the pudding hot, or cool to room temperature and then refrigerate and serve chilled.

Serves *4*
Preparation Time: *5 minutes*
Cooking Time: *10 minutes*

4 cups (1 liter) milk
2 tablespoons plus 2 teaspoons *sahlab* powder mix
   (or 2 tablespoons plus 2 teaspoons cornstarch and
   ½ teaspoon orange blossom water)
4 tablespoons sugar
1 tablespoon shelled pistachios, finely chopped
1 tablespoon unsweetened, desiccated coconut
A couple of pinches of cinnamon

1 Measure out ¼ cup (65 ml) of milk; whisk it together with the *sahlab* powder in a small bowl.
2 Whisk together the remaining milk, *sahlab*/milk mix, and sugar in a medium, heavy-bottomed saucepan. Bring to a boil over medium heat, whisking frequently; boil 2 minutes, whisking constantly.
3 Pour into 4 individual serving glasses and sprinkle the pistachio, coconut, and cinnamon on top; serve immediately.

Fresh Limeade

LIMONADA

On a hot summer day, it doesn't get any more refreshing than this. My husband remembers his mom making this for him in the throes of summer, sometimes freezing it until it had a semi-frozen icy texture, similar to Italian Granita.

Serves *8*
Preparation Time: *10 minutes*

1 batch Scented Sugar Syrup (page 28)
1½ cups (375 ml) fresh lime juice (from about
 10-12 Persian limes)
6 cups (1.5 liters) water (more or less to taste)
Sliced lime or fresh mint sprigs (optional, for garnish)

1 Prepare the Scented Sugar Syrup and stir together with the lime juice, and water in a large pitcher.
2 Serve chilled garnished with sliced lime or fresh mint, if using.

Rose Syrup Punch

SHARAB AL WARD

This fragrant syrup is used to make a very unique drink; maybe not surprisingly, it is much more a favorite with women than men.

Yields *a little over 1 cup (250 ml) of syrup*
Preparation Time: *2 minutes*
Cooking Time: *10 minutes*

1 cup (225 g) sugar
½ cup (125 ml) water
½ tablespoon fresh lemon juice
¼ cup (65 ml) rosewater
¼ teaspoon pomegranate molasses for coloring

1 Add the sugar, water, and lemon juice to a medium, thick-bottomed saucepan, and bring it to a boil over medium heat, giving the pan an occasional swirl and skimming off any foam on the surface.
2 Turn the heat down and simmer for 5 minutes, stirring occasionally. Add the rose water, turn heat up to moderately high, and cook for 2 minutes more.
3 Turn off the heat and stir in pomegranate molasses. Cool to room temperature and then store in the fridge.
4 To serve, dilute with cold water to taste (about 1 to 2 tablespoons of syrup per 1 cup/125 ml of water); add ice if desired.

Tamarind Juice Drink

ASEER TAMAR HINDI

Tamarind, which literally means "Indian Date," has a complex sweet and sour flavor that is generally more sour than sweet. This drink is incredibly refreshing with a taste reminiscent of lemonade, but with many more subtle flavor notes.

Yields *3 cups (750 ml) of syrup*
Preparation Time: *35 minutes, plus 12 hours for the tamarind to soak*
Cooking Time: *20 minutes*

½ cup (200 g) tamarind paste, cubed if in block form
4 cups (1 liter) water
2 cups (450 g) sugar

1 Combine the tamarind paste and water in a medium bowl and let it sit for 12 hours.
2 Bring the tamarind paste and the water it was soaked in to a boil in a medium saucepan over high heat; boil for 5 minutes, skimming off any foam from the top. Cool 30 minutes, then strain the liquid through a fine mesh sieve lined with cheesecloth, squeezing the cheesecloth to extract all the liquid.
3 Bring the strained liquid and sugar to a boil in a medium saucepan over medium heat; turn the heat down and simmer 5 minutes.
4 Cool the syrup to room temperature, then store refrigerated.
5 To serve, dilute with cold water to taste (about a 1:1 ratio) and pour over ice.

Tangy Yogurt Drink

LABAN AYRAAN

If you're not used to this drink, the first time you have it will likely make you pucker. Drink on though, because it gets better with each sip. This drink is salty with a refreshing tang; although garlic is optional, it gives the drink great flavor. It's usually enjoyed with heavy meals like Spiced Shawarma Chicken Wraps (page 92) or Roasted Chicken with Flatbread (page 97) since it's thought to settle the stomach.

Serves *2*
Preparation Time: *2 minutes*

2 cups (500 ml) plain yogurt
1 cup (250 ml) water
½ teaspoon salt
2 cloves garlic (optional)

1 Blend all ingredients in a blender or food processor.
2 Serve chilled.

Apricot Drink

QAMAR AL DEEN

I remember being in my mother-in-law's Syrian kitchen and seeing stack upon stack of apricot leather. This is a common sight in the Middle East, where apricots are frequently preserved by being made into leather or jam. Apricot leather can be used to make drinks, puddings, or eaten as candy, but this recipe is a favorite. This drink is very thick, with a refreshing sweet/tart flavor.

Serves *4*
Preparation Time: *10 minutes, plus 2 to 12 hours for the apricot leather to soak*

3 cups (750 ml) hot water
3 tablespoons sugar
½ lb (250 g) apricot leather (*qamar al deen*) **or dried apricots, torn or chopped into pieces**
1 teaspoon orange blossom water (optional)
Ice cubes (optional, for serving)

1 Combine the water and sugar in a large measuring cup with a pour spout, stirring until the sugar is completely dissolved.
2 Put the apricot leather into a large bowl and pour the sugar water on top. Cover, and let sit 2 to 12 hours, stirring occasionally.
3 Pour the apricot leather and water into a blender or food processor and purée with the orange blossom water, if using; strain through a fine mesh sieve.
4 Refrigerate until chilled; serve with ice, if using.

Sage Tea   SHAI MARAMIEH

Tea in the Middle East is rarely drunk as is. Instead, herbs, spices, and/or flowers like jasmine, mint, or sage are used to flavor it. Sage tea is particularly useful to drink after a meal, as it is said to soothe the stomach and aid digestion.

Serves *2*
Preparation Time: *1 minute*
Cooking Time: *5 minutes*

2 cups (500 ml) water
1 teaspoon dried sage leaves
2 teaspoons sugar
1 black tea bag

1 Pour the water and sage into a small pot; bring to a boil over medium-low heat, stirring occasionally.
2 Turn off the heat; add the sugar and stir until fully dissolved.
3 Add the black tea and steep 2 minutes.
4 Strain the tea to remove sage leaves; serve.

Turkish Coffee

QAWEH TURKIYEH

In the Middle East, two methods of coffee brewing are commonly used: the traditional Arabic method, which is generally reserved for special occasions, and the Turkish method, which is for everyday coffee. For more information, see Serving Coffee the Middle Eastern Way (page 15) and Middle Eastern Coffee Pot (page 16).

Turkish coffee is strong, rich, and velvety smooth. To make it, roasted coffee beans are ground into a fine powder with green cardamom, which gives the coffee a very distinctive flavor and aroma. The coffee is boiled with water in a special pot, and then served in very small demitasse cups, known as *fenajeen* (singular, *finjan*). The grinds aren't filtered out; rather, the dregs settle to the bottom of the cup.

Certain foods or dishes have symbolic significance across the world and coffee is the perfect example of this. In the Middle East, coffee is served to guests toward the end of their visit. It's basically a nice way for the host to ask the guests to leave without having to say it in so many words. A few years ago when Mike and I were staying with his family in Syria, there was a guest that showed up unannounced for a visit. As custom goes, my mother- and sister-in-law served him all manner of teas and sweets in what seemed like an endless procession of food. All the while Mike and I (and the rest of his family) were waiting for the guest to leave, since we had previous plans that had been interrupted. After a couple hours of eating, drinking, and talking, I pulled Mike aside and asked him how much longer he thought the guest would stay; Mike told me that his mom was making coffee, and he explained that coffee signifies to the guest that it's time to leave. And he was right, the guest was gone within the half hour.

Serves *4*
Preparation Time: *1 minute*
Cooking Time: *8 minutes*

1½ cups (375 ml) water
2 teaspoons sugar (more or less to taste)
2-3 tablespoons Turkish-ground coffee (to taste)

1 Add the water to a 2-cup (500 ml) Turkish coffee pot; bring to a boil over high heat.
2 Stir in the sugar and bring it back up to a boil.
3 Stir in the coffee off the heat, then reduce heat to low and cook until the coffee foams up, gently stirring the coffee at the top of the pot constantly. Use a spoon to scoop some of the foam off the top and transfer to the serving cups, if desired.
4 Remove from the heat and gently stir the coffee at the top until the foam goes down, then put it back on the heat and let it foam up a second time, stirring constantly.
5 Remove from the heat and stir until the foam goes down, then put it back on the heat for 3 seconds.
6 Serve immediately.

White Coffee

QAWEH BAYDA

This elegant, perfumed drink, which actually isn't coffee at all, is perfect for sipping with sweets after dinner.

Serves *2*
Preparation Time: *2 minutes*
Cooking Time: *5 minutes*

2 cups (500 ml) water
A couple of small pieces of orange peel (optional)
2 teaspoons sugar
4 teaspoons orange blossom water

1 Pour the water into a small pot and add the orange peel, if using; bring to a boil over medium-low heat, stirring occasionally.
2 Turn off the heat; add the sugar and stir until fully dissolved.
3 Stir in the orange blossom water.

⊸Middle Eastern Grocery Stores⊷

AUSTRALIA

A1 Bakery
643 Sydney Road
Brunswick, VIC 3056
Tel: 03.9386.0440

BAS Foods
423 Victoria Street
Brunswick, VIC 3056
Tel: 03.9381.1444

Cedar Bakery
33/37 High Street
Preston, VIC 3072
Tel: 03.9484.4999

Charkas
816/818 Sydney Road
Brunswick, VIC 3056
Tel: 03.9383.4487

Middle East Bakeries
20 Hope Street
Brunswick, VIC 3056
Tel: 03.9388.1044

NSM Importers & Wholesalers
Locations: Original Fruit and
Nut Shop, 23 Mary Street,
Preston, VIC 3072; NSM Conti-
nental Grocer Shop,
17 Victoria Street, Coburg, VIC
3058; Nuts About Life Shop, 2/4
Coburg Market, 415/425 Sydney
Road, Coburg, VIC 3058; Nuts
About Life, 339 Lygon Street,
Carlton, VIC 3053; NSM Direct to
Public Outlet and Showroom, 381
Victoria Street, Brunswick, VIC
3056
Tel: 93808789
Fax: 93876013
Email: omar@nsm.com.au or rita@
nsm.com.au
Website: www.nsm.com.au

Oasis Bakery
9/993 North Road
Murrumbeena, VIC 3163
Tel: 03.9570.1122

CANADA

Akhavan Supermarkets
6170 Sherbrooke W
Montréal, QC
H4B 1L8
Tel: 514.485.4887
Fax: 514.485.7009
Email: info@akhavanfood.com
Website: www.akhavanfood.com

Ararat Specialty Foods
1800 Avenue Road
North York, ON
M5M 3Z1
Tel: 416.782.5722

Arz Bakery/Fine Foods
1909 Lawrence Avenue E
Scarborough, ON
M1R 2Y6
Tel: 416.755.5084
Email: info@arzbakery.com
Website: www.arzbakery.com

Basha Foods International
2717 Sunridge Way NE
Calgary, AB
T1Y 7K7
Tel: 403.280.6797
Email: contact@bashafoods.ca
Website: bashafoods.ca

Elsafadi Brothers Super Market
11316 134 Avenue NW
Edmonton, AB
T5E 1K5
Tel: 780.475.4909

Mediterranean Bakery & Pastries
2698 Alta Vista Drive
Ottawa, ON
K1P 5K9
Tel: 613.523.2999

Mediterranean Specialty Foods
1824 Commercial Drive
Vancouver, BC
V5N 4A5
Tel: 604.438.4033

Shiraz Grocery Store
607 Somerset Street West
Ottawa, ON
K1R 5K1
Tel: 613.563.1207

EUROPE

Al Auras Shop
16 North Frederick Street
Dublin 1, Ireland
Tel: 01.887.4402

Alimentación Carnicería Halal
Calle de Lavapiés, 35
28012 Madrid, Spain

Alto Food
66 Middle Abbey Street
Dublin 1, Ireland
Tel: 01.873.3991

Auchan La Défense
2 Le Parvis de La Défense
92800 Puteaux, France
Tel: 01.41.02.30.30

Bolu-Spandau
Wilhelmstraße 3
D-10963 Berlin, Germany
Tel: 30.339.393.00
Fax: 30.339.393.02
Website:
www.bolu-lebensmittel.de

Boucherie des Passerelles
2 Rue Marcel Pagnol
95110 Sannois, France
Tel: 11.34.37.33.12

Butcher Saida
Via Principe Amedeo, 98
I-00185 Rome, Italy
Tel: 06.444.0435

Habibi
Mi ska 4/6
Warsaw, Poland
Tel: 022.435.31.55
Website: www.habibi.pl

Hal'shop
79 Rue Maurice Thorez
92000 Nanterre, France
Tel: 01.47.24.72.01

J & D Saluhall
Rinkebysvängen 61
163 74 Spånga, Sweden
Tel: 08.36.90.96
Fax: 08.36.91.80

Kamel Halal Meat Sàrl Boucherie
55 Rue de Lausanne
CH-1202 Geneva, Switzerland
Tel: 022.732.86.25

Yeni Bolu
Müllerstraße 144
D-13353 Berlin, Germany
Tel: 30.45493851

NEW ZEALAND

New Taste
142 Riddiford Street
Newtown, Wellington 6021,
New Zealand
Tel: 04.389.6070

Wellington Halal Meat
155A Riddiford Street
Newtown, Wellington 6021,
New Zealand
Tel: 04.380.0900

UNITED KINGDOM

Bismillah Food Store
3 Nicolson Square
Edinburgh, Midlothian
EH8 9BH
Tel: 0131.662.4308

Arabica Food & Spice Company
Unit 257 Grosvenor Terrace
London SE5 ONP
Locations: Borough Market, Lon-
don's Larder; Broadway Market,
Hackney;
Real Food Market, Southbank
Centre Square
Tel: 020.7708.5577
Email: info@arabicafoodandspice.
com
Website: www.arabica-
foodandspice.com

Damas Gate
81 Uxbridge Road
London W12 8NR
Tel: 020.8743.5116

Deepak Foods
953-959 Garratt Lane
London SW17 0LR
Tel: 020.8767.7819
Website: www.asianfoods.co.uk

Green Valley
36-37 Upper Berkeley Street
London W1H 5QF
Tel: 020.7402.7385

Maqbool's
36 Potterrow
Edinburgh EH8 9BT
Tel: 800.3344.3355

Phoenicia Mediterranean Food Hall
186-192 Kentish Town Road
London NW5 2AE
Tel: 020.7267.1267
E-mail: info@phoeniciafoodhall.co.uk
www.phoeniciafoodhall.co.uk

UNITED STATES

Altayebat Market
1217 S Brookhurst Street
Anaheim, CA 92804
Tel: 714.520.4723
Fax: 714.535.8540
Email: mail@altayebat.com
Website: altayebat.com

Babylon Foods
6609 Orchard Lake Road
West Bloomfield, MI 48322
Tel: 248.851.4343

Babylon Market Middle Eastern & International Food
3954 East Speedway Boulevard
Tucson, AZ, 85712
Tel: 520.232.3700
Fax: 520.207.6630
Email: F_rashid@msn.com
Website: babylonmarkettucson.com

Baiz Market
523 N 20th Street
Phoenix, AZ 85006
Tel: 602.252.8996
Fax: 602.252.8173
Website: www.baizmarket.com

Baraka Mediterranean Bakery & Cuisine
5596 Nolensville Pike
Nashville, TN 37246
Tel: 615.333.9285
Fax: 615.837.8541

Baroody Imports, Inc.
1500 B Main Avenue
Clifton, NJ 07011
Tel: 973.340.4832
Fax: 973.340.5193
Email: baroodyimports@gmail.com
Website: www.baroodyimports.com

International Food Supply
8005 SE Stark Street
Portland, Oregon 97125
Tel: 503.256.9576
Website: www.internationalfood-supply.com

Islamic Village Market
10631 Dix Avenue
Dearborn, MI 48120
Tel: 313.843.1225

Jerusalem International Foods
5360 N. Mesa St.
El Paso, TX
Tel: 915.231.9600

Kalustyan's
Marhaba International, Inc.
123 Lexington Avenue
New York, NY 10016
Toll-Free (Inside U.S. only):
800.352.3451
Tel: 212.685.3451
Fax: 212.683.8458
Email: sales@kalustyans.com
Website: www.kalustyans.com

Mediterranean Bakery & Deli
9004 Quioccasin Road
Richmond, VA 23229
Tel: 804.754.8895
Email: medbakeryanddeli@gmail.com
Website: www.mediterraneanbak-eryanddeli.net

Mediterranean Bakery & Sandwich
3362 Chamblee-Tucker Road
Atlanta, GA 30341
Tel: 770.220.0706
Email: info@mediterranean-bakery.com
Website: www.mediterranean-bakery.com

Middle East Bakery & Grocery
1512 West Foster Avenue
Chicago, IL 60640
Tel: 773.561.2224
Fax: 773.561.2234
Email: admin@middleeastbakery-andgrocery.com
Website: middleeastbakeryandgro-cery.com

Middle East Market
2254 South Colorado Boulevard
Denver, CO 80222
Tel: 303.756.4580
Fax: 303.756.1226

Phoenicia Specialty Foods
12141 Westheimer Road
Houston, TX 77077
Tel: 281.558.8225
Fax: 281.584.9912
Email: info@phoeniciafoods.com
Website: phoeniciafoods.com

Sabb's Market of Norwood
Dean Street Plaza
1001 Providence Highway
Norwood, MA 02062
Tel: 781.440.0063
Fax: 781.440.0072
Email: mail@sabmarket.com
Website: www.sabmarket.com

Sahadi's
187 Atlantic Avenue
Brooklyn, NY 11201
Tel: 718.624.4550
Fax: 718.643.4415
Email: mail@sahadis.com
Website: sahadis.com

Salim's Middle Eastern Groceries
4705 Centre Avenue
Pittsburgh, PA 15213
Tel: 412.621.8110
Fax: **412.621.8110**
Email: seltahch@hotmail.com
Website: www.salimsfoods.com

Samiramis Imports
2990 Mission Street
San Francisco, CA 94110
Tel: 415.824.6555
Fax: 415.824.6556

Season's Fresh Market
1757 N. University Drive
Plantation, FL 33322
Tel: 954.577-8626
Fax: 954.577.9343
Email: seasonsfresh@bellsouth.net
Website: seasonsfreshmarket.com

The Souk
1916 Pike Place #11
Seattle, WA 98101
Tel: 206.441.1666
Fax: 206.956.9387

The Spice House – Chicago, IL
1512 North Wells Street
Chicago, IL 60610
Tel: 312.274.0378
Email: spices@thespicehouse.com
Website: www.thespicehouse.com

The Spice House – Milwaukee, WI
Milwaukee Public Market
400 North Water Street
Milwaukee, WI 53202
Tel: 414.431.0835
Email: spices@thespicehouse.com
Website: www.thespicehouse.com

ONLINE

Buy Lebanese
Website: www.buylebanese.com

Dayna's Market
Website: daynasmarket.com

eYasmeen.com
Website: www.eyasmeen.com

Hashems
Website: www.hashems.com

Kalamala
Website: www.kalamala.com

Lebanon Mart
Website: www.lebanonmart.com

Shamra
Website: www.shamra.com

Zamouri Spices
Website: www.zamourispices.com

❧Index❧

Acknowledgments

First and foremost, all thanks to God for this opportunity. A heartfelt thanks goes to my mother-in-law, Sahar; without her beautiful *nefus ala el ekel* and willingness to teach me the art of Middle Eastern cooking this book wouldn't exist. Thanks to my parents Elizabeth and Donald who have always encouraged me to follow my dreams. Thanks to my patient husband Mike who not only willingly ate every recipe I made for this book, but also supported me through a career change, cheering me on the entire time. Thanks to my father-in-law Abraham for sharing his knowledge and for his help with translation. Thanks to Hussein for showing me around a Middle Eastern kitchen and sharing his expertise. Thanks to Rhanda and Zahra for sharing bits of Middle Eastern cuisine and culture with me. Thanks to Tareq and Noor for opening their Middle Eastern kitchen and their hearts to me. Thanks to my recipe testers, including, Ellen Trotta, Nihal Oguz, Cathy Pezzino, and especially Lynn Smith. Thanks to all who shared countless meals with Mike and I as I wrote this book, especially Marco, Erika, Donny, Rosie, and Rachel. Thanks to the author of my foreword, Lorraine Elliott (www.NotQuiteNigella.com), my blog "sister," mentor, and dear friend although we've never met in person. Thanks to my blogging friends who previewed my book, including Hannah Kaminsky (www.BitterSweetBlog.wordpress.com), Kath Younger (www.KathEats.com), and Carolyn Jung (www.FoodGal.com). Thanks to the blogging community and especially my treasured readers of An Edible Mosaic; I wrote this book with you in mind and I hope the recipes in it bring you as much joy as they do me. Special thanks to NH. Thanks to my editor, Bud Sperry, as well as the rest of the talented team at Tuttle Publishing.

The Tuttle Story: Books to Span the East and West

Most people are surprised to learn that the world's largest publisher of books on Asia had its humble beginnings in the tiny American state of Vermont. The company's founder, Charles E. Tuttle, belonged to a New England family steeped in publishing. And his first love was naturally books—especially old and rare editions.

Immediately after WW II, serving in Tokyo under General Douglas MacArthur, Tuttle was tasked with reviving the Japanese publishing industry. He later founded the Charles E. Tuttle Publishing Company, which thrives today as one of the world's leading independent publishers.

Though a westerner, Tuttle was hugely instrumental in bringing a knowledge of Japan and Asia to a world hungry for information about the East. By the time of his death in 1993, Tuttle had published over 6,000 books on Asian culture, history and art—a legacy honored by the Japanese emperor with the "Order of the Sacred Treasure," the highest tribute Japan can bestow upon a non-Japanese.

With a backlist of 1,500 titles, Tuttle Publishing is more active today than at any time in its past—inspired by Charles Tuttle's core mission to publish fine books to span the East and West and provide a greater understanding of each.

Published by Tuttle Publishing, an imprint of Periplus Editions (HK) Ltd.

www.tuttlepublishing.com

Copyright © 2012 Faith E. Gorsky

Library of Congress Cataloging-in-Publication Data
Gorsky, Faith E.
  An edible mosaic : Middle Eastern fare with extraordinary flair / Faith E. Gorsky.
     pages cm
  Includes index.
    ISBN 978-0-8048-4276-1 (hardback)
  1. Cooking, Middle Eastern. I. Title.
  TX725.M628G67 2012
  641.5956--dc23
                                    2011052446
ISBN 978-0-8048-4276-1

Distributed by

North America, Latin America & Europe
Tuttle Publishing
364 Innovation Drive
North Clarendon, VT 05759-9436 U.S.A.
Tel: 1 (802) 773-8930; Fax: 1 (802) 773-6993
info@tuttlepublishing.com
www.tuttlepublishing.com

Japan
Tuttle Publishing
Yaekari Building, 3rd Floor
5-4-12 Osaki, Shinagawa-ku
Tokyo 141 0032
Tel: (81) 3 5437-0171; Fax: (81) 3 5437-0755
sales@tuttle.co.jp
www.tuttle.co.jp

Asia Pacific
Berkeley Books Pte. Ltd.
61 Tai Seng Avenue, #02-12
Singapore 534167
Tel: (65) 6280-1330; Fax: (65) 6280-6290
inquiries@periplus.com.sg
www.periplus.com

15 14 13 12   10 9 8 7 6 5 4 3 2 1

Printed in Hong Kong   1209 EP

OCT — 2013